THE SPORTING LIFE

HOW TO HELP YOURSELF WITH HOODOO FROM THE STREETS TO THE SHEETS

PROFESSOR CHARLES PORTERFIELD

Lucky Mojo Curio Company
Forestville, California

→ 2016 ←

Text:
Charles Porterfield, with catherine yronwode

Art:
Charles Dawson, Nelson Hahne, P. Craig Russell, Steve Leialoha, Trina Robbins,
Leslie Cabarga, catherine yronwode, one Unknown Artist, and Grey Townsend

Cover:
Charles Dawson and Grey Townsend, with Trina Robbins

Editor:
catherine yronwode

Production:
catherine yronwode, nagasiva yronwode, and Charles Porterfield

First Edition 2016, Second Edition 2019

Published by
Lucky Mojo Curio Company
6632 Covey Road,
Forestville, California 95436
LuckyMojo.com

ISBN: 978-0-9961471-2-5

Printed in Canada.

CONTENTS

Dedication.. 4
Acknowledgement 4
Preface 5
Hoodoo, Conjure, and Rootwork 7
    What Hoodoo Is 7
    What Hoodoo Is Not 7
What is the Sporting Life? 8
    Slinging Slang 9
Working Girls and Hustling Women 14
    Fancy Ladies, Call Girls, and Hookers 14
    Madams and Aunties 18
    Spells for Prostitutes and Escorts................................... 20
Flesh Peddlers and Gentlemen of Leisure 26
    Pimps, Loverboys, and Sugar Daddies 26
    Bringing Them In and Turning Them Out 30
    Spells for Procurers and Panderers 32
Sissy Men and Bull Dagger Women 38
    Boy-Girls, Queers, and Drag Queens 38
    You Sure Gotta Prove It On Me 42
    Spells for Gay Men and Lesbian Women 44
Gamblers, Runners, and Players 50
    Policy and the Numbers 50
    Beating the Odds 54
    Spells for Games of Chance and Skill 56
Bootleggers, Traffickers, and Pushers 62
    To Live Outside the Law You Must Be Honest 62
    Keeping The Man Away 66
    Spells for Breaking the Rules While Staying Safe 68
Dives, Houses, and Holes 74
    Brothels and Cathouses 74
    The Juke Joint 79
    Spells for Drawing Trade to an Illegal Business 81
Dressing for the Demimonde 86
    Nice Shoes and the Walking Blues 86
    Hide My Eyes 89
    Spells for Looking Good and Staying Sharp 92
Bibliography 96

DEDICATION

This is for all those who worked behind the scarlet curtain, on the street, or under the red light, at the track, laying out the odds, or watching the policy shop, as well as Henry J. Wehman, Professor Uriah Konje (Herbert Gladstone Parris), and "the master of the diminished 5th," Jelly Roll Morton (Ferdinand Joseph LaMothe).

"To All Oppressed People Of The World
To become an able and successful person in any profession two things are necessary, study and practice. The one who succeeds in life is the one who early on clearly knows his object and toward that object routinely directs his powers. Education has the magnificent quality of setting one apart from others. It can provide one with something that not only meets the needs of today, but rather the means to meet the demands of the day after tomorrow and the day after that.

Education can have as its function the changing of social status or the preservation of the status quo. The final choice lies with each and every one of us.

I am appealing to all to make the former choice."

— Professor Uriah Konje

ACKNOWLEDGEMENTS

The author would like to acknowledge the following for their contributions:
Gabrielle Swain: My mother and confidant. You cast open the proscenium arch for me and showed me the wonders, joys, and worth of the demimonde.
Christy Porterfield: This is for you, Effie darling. You're a damn good man, sister.
My sons: Rumble, young men, rumble. Pop will always be in your corners.
My grandsons: How you grow, how you grow. You will be as tall as mountains.
Catherine Yronwode: My dear friend of wise wit and sharp mind. I will never forget all you have done for me. You let me shoot the dice and take the chance.
Nagasiva Yronwode: A treatise on the night for you, my dear devilish friend.
Grey Townsend: Too far away, but close to heart. Your skill is amazing.
Khi Armand: Your kindness, attention, and generosity helped momentously.
Michele Jackson: Your clarity of vision and friendship mean so much to me.
Shaun Laveau: Thank you for your hard work and diligence. You will go far.
Particular gratitude to the Rev. Harry Middleton Hyatt, an Anglican minister and folklorist who interviewed 1,600 African-American hoodoo practitioners from 1936-1970 — and to his 1,600 interviewees. Read more about them here:
LuckyMojo.com/hyattinformants.html
Finally, thanks to the fine contributors from the Association of Independent Readers and Rootworkers, individually named with their spells. Find them here:
ReadersAndRootworkers.org

PREFACE

"One can hear all that's going on in the street. Which means that from the street one can hear what's going on in this house."

— Jean Genet

When I started this book I did not want to write a book on criminality or for criminals. Instead I desired to write about that part of hoodoo that helped those who were in professions or living lifestyles that the law or public of their times found immoral or objectionable, a world that now has often become legal and accepted — the world of the sporting life.

An intentional concealment surrounds the sporting life, and even in the realm of magic which itself can be secretive this is the real "underworld" work, as the assistant rector at the Church of the Holy Spirit, and American folklorist, Rev. Harry Middleton Hyatt called it. The realm of working girls, pimps, and gamblers remains out of the sight of the law and the supposed upright citizens, who in the end are the customers of these forbidden enterprises. This makes talking about that world out in the open a challenge or a shock to some.

How I became linked with the demimonde, or the "half-world," as the 19th century French writer Alexandre Dumas Fils named it, is an odd tale. When I first opened my practice I found that I had put several words together in public that brought those involved in the sporting life to me. Exactly what those words were still eludes me, but I suspect that they involved a particular Rooster and a certain yard. Soon I was being contacted by folks "in the life" from all over. Gamblers I had worked with before, as I had been an avid speculator of the sport of kings. In other words, I played the ponies and spent many an afternoon poring over a scratch sheet figuring out which Horse was to be my winner that day. I also had known many working girls and had good friends engaged in that profession. Now I found myself called on to counsel, read, and work not only for them, but for pimps and hustlers as well. And why not!

Hoodoo exists, in part, to assist those oppressed by or in need of help "greasing the wheel" when dealing with "The Man." Many considered me a contradiction: a worker well versed in the Bible who aided gamblers, pimps, and prostitutes. I see no conflict in this, for I feel I am with decent folk, and I am sure Jesus would approve of the company I have kept.

The work I learned involving the sporting life had to come to me as an adult. When I was young no one spoke in the open of such things around children, nor did they discuss the kind of magic used to aid it. In fact, my maternal grandmother said that one should avoid "such people" and that being an actress was just as bad as being a prostitute, if not worse, because actresses made less than working girls did!

Help in creating this book came my way from elders living and dead, as well as dear friends, and those colleagues who did similar work. I received great aid and knowledge from the Georgia worker, Mr. Charles Hanson, may his memory be a blessing, who was a lovely rascal himself. As time went on I found the issue to be so covered up, hidden, and obscured because of its subject matter that I often wanted to pull my beard out.

Whenever we talk about sex work, gambling, and other such matters there will inevitably be some who will decry it and clutch their pearls in shock. I am of a different stripe; I believe that discussions of this sort are important, for they are a part of what makes us who we are and also part of that with which hoodoo has been more than a little involved. In this opinion I enjoy the freedoms of the age I live in and need not engage in the worry that Rev. Harry M. Hyatt did when he wished to write about such matters. For this I am grateful because it allows me the freedom to share and discuss this information in a frank, open, and honest manner.

What you hold in your hands now is my small attempt to open the curtains and windows and let some light and air into a smoky room filled with dice, bottles of liquor, cigar ash, and the enticement of lovely ladies and handsome gentlemen lounging on couches of red velvet. No one book could hold all the information about the sporting life in hoodoo, but I have thrown the dice and taken my chance at hitting the good spots.

I have tried to cover as much as I could herein, from figures in the Bible to good old-fashioned spell work, and, I hope, a pleasant dose of history. This, then, is more than just a book of spells and tricks; it is my own red light in the window calling you inside to come sit, rest, taste the joie de vivre, and learn about the sporting life. So, as they say in New Orleans, *"Laissez les bons temps rouler!"*

Professor Charles Porterfield
Denton, Texas
March, 2016

HOODOO, CONJURE, AND ROOTWORK

"You must go to bed with friends or whores, where money makes up the difference in beauty or desire."

— St. Augustine

WHAT HOODOO IS

Hoodoo, also known as conjure, rootwork, tricking, helping yourself, or just "that stuff," is African–American folk magic. Made up of African magical practices imbued with Protestant Christianity, Native American herb lore, European, Jewish, Asian, and Spiritualist ideas and customs, its tools include herbs, roots, oils, washes, waters, incense, candles, and small bags called mojos, jomos, or tobies. Although it was born in the oppression of bondage this was not the flower of its tree. No, that would come later after emancipation, the great migration, and in freedom. Hoodoo is not a lost art; instead it continues to adapt, grow, and thrive. It remains an integral and vital part of American culture that still lives to this day.

WHAT HOODOO IS NOT

Hoodoo is not a traditional African religion. It is not Voodoo, West African Vodun, Candomblé, Palo, Ifa, Santería, Obeah, or Quimbanda.

Hoodoo is not Appalachian, French, or Scots-Irish folk magic.

Hoodoo is not Wicca, Neo–Paganism, or "New Age."

Hoodoo does not have initiatory rituals, and there is no hierarchy.

Hoodoo has no belief in "karma" or a "three–fold law of return."

Hoodoo is not "Black Magic" or "The Devil's Work."

Hoodoo is not a practice of "do as you please" or "as you will." It has a pattern, tradition, taste, and sound to it, just like Jazz or Southern cooking. This book is not meant to be an encouragement for the reader to just "take and run." Instead I present it as a guide and aid to help the reader go out and "cook good Southern food and play great Jazz."

For more on the history of hoodoo see:

- **LuckyMojo.com/hoodoohistory.html**
- **Southern-Spirits.com**
- **LuckyMojo.com/hoodooandreligion.html**

WHAT IS THE SPORTING LIFE?

"I went into the sporting life for business reasons … I considered myself then and I do now — as a businesswoman."

— Mattie Silks

As we begin this book about the sporting life we need to stop for a moment and first ask an important question: What is the sporting life?

The term is not often heard these days, and a good number of people have no idea what it means when they hear "the sporting life." Some think that it is a reference to physical sports, but it has little to do with team sports or similar pursuits except as a part of its early history.

The phrase has had an interesting evolution. It began as a way to describe appropriate physical activities, such as hunting and amateur boxing, which supposedly benefited the Victorian male both physically and morally. However, it soon began to change in meaning. "The outdoor life" came to describe healthy sports, while, particularly in the United States, sporting games were associated with gambling, prostitution, and the allegedly physically and morally unhealthy "city life," because athletic and sporting events were occasions for drinking in saloons where betting on sports events, other sorts of gambling, and consorting with "loose women" all united. By the 1830s "a sporting gentleman" had come to mean a gambler. In the 1850s "a sporting house" was an establishment that catered to gamblers and drinkers; by the 1870s the phrase blatantly meant a brothel. By then a "sporting lady" was a prostitute in a brothel, and a "sportsman," or "sport," was an ardent gambler, drinker, and frequent patron of the brothels.

The sporting life, of course, had its highs and lows, reflecting the social class and affluence of those involved in it. The most affluent frequented the best clubs, saloons, gambling houses, and brothels, most within walking distance of big and luxurious hotels. The more modest to lower class clubs emphasised drinking and gambling in establishments "below the line" or "on the wrong side of the tracks." By the 1860s "sportsmen" in this strata were in great attendance at Dog, Rat, and Cock fights, Horse races, and boxing matches, especially those held inside the saloons. In time the sporting life evolved into a catch-all term which included homosexuals, artists, free thinkers, radicals, and all those who lived or worked in the world of the night or on the other side of the law.

SLINGING SLANG

The language of the sporting life, like any form of cant, is constantly changing. African-Americans in "the life" not only held onto words from African languages such as Wolof, Ki-Kongo, and Bantu, they also retained bits of Elizabethan English long after such words disappeared from White vocabularies. As a form of code, such slang allows those in the life to speak freely around those not hip without "outing" themselves.

- **Bag:** Your bag is what you do, what motivates and excites you. "Coming out of a bag" means to verbally or physically assault someone.
- **B.D. Woman / Bull Dagger / Bull Dyke:** Also a "tush-hog" or "bo' hog" woman. A masculine identifying lesbian. Bull dagging is lesbian sex.
- **Biscuit:** A reference to sex. A skilled male or female lover is a "biscuit roller." In the 1930s and '40s biscuit also sometimes referred to a skull.
- **Boogie:** Your butt. To shake your butt, dance vigorously, or have sexual intercourse. Possibly from the Bantu word *mbuki*, meaning to dance.
- **Booting:** Having sexual intercourse. Bootlegging. Enjoying the immediate effects of a narcotic injection by injecting it little by little.
- **Bootleg:** Illicit liquor, usually whiskey. Adulterated coffee, usually mixed with Chicory. A bootlegger. Any illicit article of trade.
- **Bootlegger:** A smuggler or manufacturer of illicit liquor. Also, from the 1940s on, one who violates the copyrights of books, records, or tapes.
- **Bottom Girl:** A prostitute who serves as office manager for her pimp, collecting money and keeping the pimp apprised of police activity.
- **Cabbage:** Female genitalia, as in *"good cabbage for sale."* Other terms for this include cake, jellyroll, muffin, fish, cooter, coochie, and pie.
- **Call Girl:** A sex worker, often one employed by a so-called escort agency. The client must call by telephone to arrange a date with her.
- **Cat:** Another person who you respect. Possibly from the Wolof word for a singer, *katt*, as well as the Wolof suffix *–kat*, meaning a person.
- **Cathouse:** A brothel. Dore DuFran, a madam in Deadwood, South Dakota, coined the term in reference to her own brothel.
- **Checkerboard:** Interracial relationships or one in such, as in *"she's a checkerboard chick,"* or *"a checkerboard band."* The local corner bar.
- **Chick:** The Wolof word *jigen* meant an attractive young woman. By the 1920s it united with "chicken," becoming chick: a sexy young woman.

- **Chicken:** A child, teen, or underage partner, generally either a young woman or a young homosexual male; also synonymous with pussy.
- **Chicken Hawk:** A pedophile; a man who sexually abuses young boys or girls; after raping them he may also force them into prostitution.
- **Choosing Up:** When one pimp takes "ownership" of a girl from another pimp. Also when a girl chooses a man to be her pimp.
- **Chump:** A person who is an easy victim, easy dupe, or a mark; a loser. May come from "chum," a prison term from the 1600s for a cellmate.
- **Cock:** Black term for female genitalia, from the low English "to copulate." To "cock it on the wall," is to have sex while standing up and leaning against a wall. In White slang, a cock is a penis; Blacks call that a "dick."
- **Cool:** The ability to remain calm, generous, and confident. Among the Yoruba, connecting to one's inner divinity manifests as a coolness.
- **Date:** The activity of prostitution. A client is "with a date" or "dating." Men may hire a "date" to provide them with "a girlfriend experience."
- **Dig:** To "get," understand, or appreciate something. Possibly from the Wolof *deg*, meaning to understand, call attention to, or appreciate.
- **Dog:** In Southern Nigeria someone who is oversexed is called a Dog. An oversexed, infidelitous, devious, or scheming man. An ugly woman.
- **Easeman:** A man who lives a life of ease, earns "easy money," and lives on "Easy Street"; a pimp. *"Natural-born easemen don't have to work."*
- **Family / Folks:** Those under the control of one pimp. He plays the role of "father" while the group fulfills the role of "family." See Stable.
- **Fix:** To rig a game or competition. To prepare an item or affect a person with a magical spell. A shot of drugs to prevent withdrawal symptoms.
- **Funk / funky:** From the Ki-Kongo word *lu-funki*, meaning bad body odour. An athletic dance that makes you sweat. Dance music itself.
- **Fuzz:** The police. Possibly from the Wolof word *fas*, for Horse, because African slaves observed police mounted on horseback.
- **Gentleman of Leisure:** A pimp, playboy, gigolo, or professional gambler. A man who has irregular or illegal sources of income.
- **Gold Digger / Kept Woman / Lothario:** A woman or man who enters into long-term personal relationships to obtain money or status.
- **Grind:** To rotate the pelvis during sex. A sexual adept is a "coffee grinder" or "mill man," referring to a grist mill. Your job is also a grind.
- **Hip:** To know what is going on around you. Traced to the Wolof word *hipi*, meaning to open one's eyes or to be aware of what is going on.

- **Hooker:** A prostitute, often a streetwalker, who hooks, catches, or snares her clients off the street into alleys or hourly rent rooms.
- **Hoochie-coochie:** Hoochie is a whore, coochie a vagina. Hoochie-coochie dancers are strippers; a hoochie-coochie man is a pimp.
- **Hustling / Hustler:** Prostitutes soliciting clients; a prostitute. Also to obtain money by gambling, grifting, or begging; or one who does so.
- **Jake:** Liquor made with Jamaica Ginger. During Prohibition, solvent-adulterated Jake led to neurological damage. Also good or satisfactory.
- **Jazzing:** To have sexual intercourse. African-American slang related to "jasm," "jism," and "jizz" (semen). Jazz music is lascivious music.
- **Jive:** Language that is either coded or deliberately misleading. Related to the Wolof word *jev*, meaning to talk disparagingly about someone.
- **John:** An individual, almost always male, who pays for or trades something of value for sex acts from a prostitute. Also known as a trick.
- **Lemon:** The sex organ of either a female or male. A woman might "squeeze your lemon," or she might say that a man did the same to her.
- **Life, the:** The sporting life, "the game," "the racket." A socially scorned lifestyle of gambling, bootlegging, female impersonation, or prostitution.
- **Madam:** A woman who runs a brothel, escort service, or "house of ill repute." She may work alone or with others; her employees are "girls."
- **Mark:** The subject of a con. The intended victim of a swindler, hustler, or cardsharp. Usually a person who lacks street smarts.
- **Model / Stripper / Cam Girl / Phone Sex Operator:** One who disrobes, poses, dances, or simulates sex acts for pay, but does not touch clients.
- **Pick-Up Artist / PUA:** One who specializes in the rapid seduction of sexual parters, usually in public venues, by means of studied techniques.
- **Pussy:** Female genitalia. Related terns are "cathouse," and "a belly [or barrel] full of kittens." Also a weak or effeminate-seeming man.
- **Rambling:** To go from place to place without settling down; a feckless avoidance of work and family responsibility. Also sexual voraciousness.
- **Rap:** To talk, converse, tease, or speak. A type of spoken song. To steal a purse. An arrest or conviction. A "rap sheet" is a list of convictions.
- **Red-Light District:** A part of a city where one finds prostitutes and brothels, thus called from the red lights once used as signs for brothels.
- **Reefer:** The Marijuana plant; also tea, muggles, hemp, pot, Mary Jane, dope, jive, mez, weed. A Marijuana cigarette is a joint, stick, reefer, or blunt. A Marijuana smoker is a viper, a tea-head, or simply a head.

- **Rider:** One's sexual partner or steady lover. Riding is having sexual intercourse. Riding "with the saddle on" is using a condom during sex.
- **Rock and Roll:** To have sexual intercourse. Rock is a reciprocal motion, roll is a circular motion. *"My daddy rocks me with one steady roll."*
- **Runner:** Someone who carries, smuggles, or transports illegal goods, whether drugs, betting numbers, bootleg liquor, or stolen merchandise.
- **Saltwater:** Alcohol. A "salty" person or one who "jumps salty" is irritated or annoyed, or is an aggressive and tough veteran or prisoner.
- **Score:** A grievance that requires satisfaction. Securing an advantage. Buying illicit substances. A successful robbery. A sexual conquest.
- **Shake:** A rent party (1920s); an erotic "Oriental" dance (1930s). Poor Marijuana, just stems and seeds. To "shake down" is to extort (1940s).
- **Shave / Shave 'Em Dry:** To shave is to grind so hard as to rub away pubic hair. To shave 'em dry is quick sex without female arousal or lubrication.
- **Shimmy:** A popular dance from the 1800s to the 1930s, also called the Shimmy-She-Wobble. Named for the silky chemises that women wore.
- **Shuck:** To exaggerate, lie, or clown around. Possibly from the Bantu word *shikuka*, which means to lie, bluff, or fake, or a variant of "shit."
- **Sissy:** An effeminate-acting homosexual man. A man who engages in cross-gender or womanish behaviour. A straight man's secret male lover.
- **Stable:** A group of prostitutes who work for a single pimp, madam, brothel, or escort service. Some pimps tattoo the girls in their stable.
- **Sugar Daddy / Mama:** A wealthy man or woman who lavishes gifts on a younger partner in return for companionship, escort services, or sex.
- **Sugar Baby / Gigolo:** A young woman or man who is recompensed by a Sugar Daddy or Mama for companionship, escort services, or sex.
- **Tomie / Tonie / Doney / Doanie:** From Spanish "doña" (lady); by the 1870s it was circus slang for a demimondaine. In Black slang, one's lover.
- **Trick:** A john. An act of prostitution. A sex worker "turns a trick" or is "with a trick." A hoodoo spell is also a "trick" and a mojo is a "trick bag."
- **Trim:** Female genitalia. It is usually used by a man to express a need or intention to get sex, as in *"I'm gonna get me some trim tonight."*
- **Turned Out:** Guided or forced into prostitution, or a person newly involved in prostitution. When someone turns another to prostitution.
- **Washboard:** A ridged board for laundering, also played with thimbles or finger picks. "Rubbing her washboard" is manually pleasing a woman.
- **Yas-Yas-Yas:** Ass. *"If you can't shake ya shoulders, shake ya yas-yas-yas."*

Spiritual Supplies for the sporting life in hoodoo catalogues, 1868 - 2016. Art by Charles Dawson, Nelson Hahne, P. Craig Russell, Steve Leialoha, Trina Robbins, Leslie Cabarga, catherine yronwode, Keith Henderson, charlie wylie, and Two Unknown Artists for E. W. Hoyt and Co.. King Novelty Co., Sovereign Products Co., Joseph E. Meyer / Indiana Herb Gardens, Lucky Mojo Curio Co., Chicago Exhibit Supply Co., and Charles Williams Shoe Co.

WORKING GIRLS AND HUSTLING WOMEN

"My girl, I appoint with you an appointment — and I charge you that you make preparation to be worthy to meet me,"

— Walt Whitman

In his 1889 story "On the City Wall," Rudyard Kipling wrote that prostitution was "the most ancient profession in the world." During the early 1900s medical professionals and others often misquoted the phrase until it became "the world's oldest profession," a title it shared with farmers, shepherds, and murderers. What constitutes prostitution is debatable, but there is evidence that other animals engage in it as well. The desires, aims, and needs of the sugar baby, gold digger, and working girl bleed over into those of the mistress, lover, and wife. Whatever the definition, the prostitute figures greatly in our history, music, literature, and film. She is the subject of frequent social debates and campaigns, but the truth of who she is remains an unresolved matter. Her place in hoodoo, though, is without debate, and she is a powerful figure within it.

FANCY LADIES, CALL GIRLS, AND HOOKERS

From the brothel to the mean streets and all points in between, the prostitute has plied her wares for kings, soldiers, farm boys, and the everyday working man. Within her own profession there is a hierarchy stretching from the glittering heights of the courtesan down to the hooker.

At the top of the ladder are the fancy lady, who receives her well-to-do clients in a high class brothel, and the call girl, who goes to meet her clients in a private location after they call ahead for her. The escort is a type of call girl who may offer an artificial "girlfriend experience" to her johns. Working girls in cathouses occupy a middle position in the hierarchy. Off to the side stand the model, stripper, phone sex operator, and cam girl who simulate intimacy without physical contact. The sexual massage parlour worker offers sexual release without intimacy. The hooker, who hooks her clients into convenient alleys or by-the-hour rent rooms, and the hard working streetwalker, who walks a beat like her ever-present foe the cop, occupy the bottom rung of this ladder. No matter the position or the clients, the rise of sex work from scorned illegality to slow acceptance is an ongoing one.

PROSTITUTION, POWER AND FREEDOM

In the 19th century a woman who had property, earned good wages, engaged in sex outside of marriage, utilized birth control, danced, drank, associated with men of other races, wore make-up, perfume, and fashionable clothes without shame or regret was probably a prostitute. Prostitutes enjoyed freedoms that most women now take for granted. In a time when females were expected to remain in the "private sphere," prostitutes travelled alone freely and boldly as "public women." They made by far the highest wages of American women. When birth control was essentially illegal, prostitutes utilized and helped manufacture and distribute contraceptives. Long before it was acceptable for women to dance in public, prostitutes helped invent many of the dance steps that later became popular during the dance crazes of 1910s and '20s. Public drinking and gambling were forbidden for women, but prostitutes were fixtures in saloons and were some of the most successful gamblers in the nation. Perhaps most ironically, the clothing, hairstyles, and make-up of prostitutes, such as lipstick — "the scarlet shame of streetwalkers," which was so maligned at one time — have now become the fashionable norm.

THE TWO-DOLLAR BILL

In hoodoo a brand new $2.00 bill is the luckiest bill one can use for matters of the sporting life or gambling, and it should always be the bill used in money spells if you can get one. The reasons for this are threefold:

First, the $2.00 bill is hard to come by, and a brand new one more so.

Second, a $2.00 bet was the lowest bet one could make at the race track, so *"betting a brand new $2.00 bill is like betting all your money on one sure thing, like you know it'll come lucky. That means you believe."*

Finally, $2.00 was once the price of the cheapest prostitutes. By the early 1960s this was no longer the case, but it was certainly true in the 1920s, as attested to by many blues songs of the time. Even today after the cost of a working girl rose, the $2.00 bill is still known as a "whore's wages."

A typical 2oth century blues song that mentions the $2.00 bill and prostitution is "Shave 'Em Dry" by Lucille Bogan, recorded in 1935:

"My back is made of whalebone,
And my cock is made of brass,
And my fuckin' is made for workin' men's two dollars,
Great God, round to kiss my ass."

FAMOUS PROSTITUTES OF THE BIBLE

The Bible is actively used in hoodoo, and the prostitute appears many times in it prominently. She has been a figure of scorn, warning, and disgrace in the Bible, but also one of virtue, love, and righteousness. Her influence has saved nations, ruined kings, and even aided the Saviour.

DELILAH [Judges 16]

The quintessential temptress of the Bible, Delilah was a woman from the valley of Sorek who became the lover and betrayer of Samson. Paid to discover the secret of Samson's strength, she became his lover and found that his power came from a Nazarite vow which precluded the cutting of his hair. Delilah had his locks cut while he slept, robbing him of his strength. Her name is a slander used against prostitutes as spreaders of venereal diseases and as women who bring men to their ruin.

In hoodoo Delilah's influence helps remove, control, or capture a man's nature and power. She is also invoked in work designed to make a man helpless and malleable to a woman's desires and designs. Wives who wish to make their husbands meek and obedient will work with her as well.

JEZEBEL [1st and 2nd Kings]

Synonymous with treachery, promiscuity, and controlling women, Jezebel was a Phoenician princess and the wife of Ahab, King of Northern Isræl. She enflamed her husband to abandon the worship of God, to worship the deities Baal and Asherah, and to persecute and kill the prophets of God. For these offenses Jezebel met a horrific end; a member of her court threw her from her window, and stray dogs consumed her corpse. Her name, "Jezebel," is also used as a slander against women of African descent, suggesting that Black women have greater sexual appetites and are more promiscuous than White women. White slave owners used this argument to justify the rape and forced procreation of their female slaves. In the 19th century the term "a painted Jezebel" was used against prostitutes and loose women. In response to this slur, women started actively reclaiming the name Jezebel with pride.

In hoodoo, sex workers and controlling women bathe with bath crystals, dust their clothes and the insoles of their shoes with sachet powders, and suffumigate their homes with incense powders all named in her honour. The Jezebel root is also used to work the Curse of Jezebel.

MARY MAGDALENE [Luke 7:36-50]

Although many believe Mary Magdalene to have been a prostitute, scripture only states that Jesus cast seven demons from her and she became his follower. She witnessed his crucifixion and was the first to see him after his resurrection. Many identify her with the woman who washed and perfumed Jesus' feet. Some suggest that she was the wife of John the Baptist or even Jesus. She is not seen much in hoodoo except in the "Latin quarters." Mary Magdalene is the patroness of sexual temptation, repentant sinners, and "wayward women." Her favourite offerings are Myrrh and Spikenard. She is prayed to or invoked to aid, protect, or redeem prostitutes.

RAHAB [Joshua 2]

Named as one of the four most beautiful women in the world, Rahab is the original "Hooker with a Heart of Gold." Rahab was a prostitute and possible madam living in the city of Jericho. She aided Joshua's spies, who promised to spare her if she marked her house by hanging a red cord out the window. This gave rise to the belief that the red cord became the red lamps of the "red-light district." After leaving Jericho and possibly marrying Joshua, Rahab became the ancestor of King David.

Jewish folklore states that one who mentions Rahab's name lusts after her. In hoodoo her name aids in lust works and with a spiritual bath of Hyssop to purify working girls, or those doing dominating lust work, of sin.

TAMAR [Genesis 38: 11 - 26]

Like Rahab, Tamar is an ancestor of Jesus. Her first two husbands, Judah's sons, were slain by God for wickedness. Denied marriage to Judah's youngest son, Tamar disguised herself as a harlot and went to him. He propositioned her, and she agreed, taking his staff, seal, and cord as a security. When Tamar became visibly pregnant Judah ordered her burned as a prostitute. Tamar sent him word the child was his with his staff, seal, and cord. Judah freed and married her. She bore him twin sons.

Tamar is called on to help women who have been scorned or denied things they were promised. She can be used to make deadbeat dads pay child support and to stop those who make false claims against women.

You can read more about the Bible in hoodoo in this book:
"Hoodoo Bible Magic" by Miss Michæle and Prof. C. D. Porterfield

MADAMS AND AUNTIES

Prostitutes who rose to the top of their profession often opened brothels and became madams. In the 19th century madams possessed more wealth, and often more property, than any other women in the United States. Although there were disparities between the races, African-American madams enjoyed the same levels of success, power, and influence as their White counterparts, and madams were among the wealthiest people in the country, especially in the South and the West.

A reoccurring character in 19th century literature about prostitution is the aunt or auntie, a madam who lured homeless or abused girls into "a life of shame." Actually, in the competitive markets of the red-light districts, which invariably had several brothels, most madams not only paid their girls better wages than could be found in other employment, but provided free birth control, health care, legal protection, housing, and meals. Few American workers of either sex enjoyed such benefits as these in the 19th century. Certainly, some madams did abuse their girls or place them into debt slavery, but these tended to be the less prosperous brothel owners.

By the middle of the 19th century the popularity and power of madams caused social reformers to warn that they were undermining the virtues of the nation. Madams were said to be *female fiends of the worst kind, who seem to have lost all the better qualities of human nature.* However, madams regularly appeared in court on their own behalf and won quite frequently.

The historian Paula Petrik has researched a large number of 19th century court cases in the West in which prostitutes brought suit to *challenge men who assaulted, robbed, or threatened them.* In half of the cases *the judge or jury found for the female complainants.* Petrik also found *a singular lack of legal and judicial concern with sexual commerce* in the period before the rise of moral reformers. This social and legal tolerance of prostitution coincided with a period in which sex workers showed little of the supposed self-destructiveness later presumed to be the norm among them. Although there was rampant use of alcohol and drugs by the prostitutes of Helena, Colorado, for example, Petrik stated that *Not one whore in Helena died by her own hand before 1883,* and there were *no reports of prostitutes dying of alcoholism or drug overdose between 1865 and 1883.* Instead, the greatest threat to a prostitute's health was — and remains — the risk of infection with a sexually transmitted disease passed along to her by a client.

HOODOO PRODUCTS FOR SEX WORKERS AND MADAMS

Many traditional hoodoo products are used by prostitutes and madams to attract and control their trade. Madams may also work to control their girls and to keep the peace among them. These products are employed in a variety of ways, such as on their bodies, clothes, bedsheets, phones, camera equipment, and in the private rooms where they do their work.

- **Attraction:** These products help draw attention to the wearer like a magnet and they make people feel enthralled and engrossed with them.
- **Bewitching:** An old hoodoo formula used in works to help create an air of mystery, fascination, allure, and sexual attraction around one.
- **Cleo May:** A well-known product for attracting tips from men, used by sex workers, waitresses, bartenders, entertainers, and card readers.
- **Come To Me:** A popular herb-based love attracting formula worn as a personal scent to draw a lover or client of the opposite sex closer.
- **Commanding:** Useful in domination love work or when one wants to be in command, lead, or enforce one's own will on those around them.
- **Domination:** Excellent for madams, dominatrixes, sugar babies, and gold diggers to help rule over and control their girls, clients, or marks.
- **Essence of Bend-Over:** Another good product for dominatrixes and madams. Used to make others obey through degradation or subjugation.
- **Follow Me Boy/Girl:** Used to attract, dominate, and hold a woman or man. Works by gender, regardless of the target's sexual orientation.
- **Geranium:** Working girls historically used this essential oil, as well as Rose Geranium, to dress their skirts and underwear to attract clients.
- **Hoyt's Cologne:** A traditional spiritual cologne used by prostitutes to bathe themselves as well as to anoint their clothes to draw in clients.
- **Jezebel:** Sex workers who use products named after Jezebel, are often prostitutes who specialize in dominating or controlling their clients.
- **Look Me Over:** Useful for casting calls, brothel line-ups, exotic dancers, or cam girls to entice prospective clients to notice them first.
- **Money Drawing:** Mixed with other products, such as in this list, it aids in bringing good wages and tips to sex workers and money to a brothel.
- **Peaceful Home:** Helpful for putting an end to strife in a brothel or to help settle disputes so that all are mutually content and co-operative.
- **Wealthy Way:** For a well-off sugar baby or working girl to bring clients to supply a stream of money to keep her in her high lifestyle.

SPELLS FOR PROSTITUTES AND ESCORTS

TO MAKE A CLIENT OR LOVER GENEROUS WITH MONEY
Fill the back of a $2.00 bill with, *"[Name], you had best be generous to me with your money."* Dress it in a five-spot pattern with Jezebel, Money Drawing, and Attraction Oils. Fold it toward you and wear it in your bra.

TO GET A MAN TO KEEP YOU WELL
A working girl or sugar baby who wants a man to keep her in good circumstances should get a Follow Me Boy vigil candle and dedicate the candle in her man's name, then recite over it Psalms 18:19: *"He brought me forth also into a large place; he delivered me, because he delighted in me."* Burn the candle during the evening hours until done.

MAKE A LOVER, PIMP, OR SUGAR DADDY GENEROUS
Miss Cat advises us that "adding Chamomile to love-drawing oils, powders, baths, perfumes, washes, or incense helps your lover to be more forthcoming with money. If a spell involves writing the name of your lover or sugar daddy on a petition, use a two-dollar bill instead of regular paper."

REV. CLARK'S LUCKY LOVE DOUCHE FOR WORKING GIRLS
"Make a tea of a handful of Rose petals, a teaspoon of honey, and a pinch each of Catnip, Chamomile, Damiana, and Licorice root. Steep it in a quart of spring water for seven minutes, stirring clockwise and reciting the 23rd Psalm. Strain the herbs out, add half a cup of Rose water, let it cool, and use it to dress your pussy or douche with as you would a commercial douche."

MISS CAT'S MACE DOUCHE TO GET REPEATERS
"Prostitutes who mix Mace powder with distilled vinegar and water say that a man whose member comes in contact with a woman who has thus dressed her pussy will seek her out and pay her well for repeated trysts."

MISS CAT'S PROSTITUTE'S AMULET TO DRAW TRADE
"Dress a Jezebel Root with Follow Me Boy Oil and your sexual fluids every day for seven days. Keep this on you or in your purse to help bring you submissive, docile clients who will not cause you any trouble and who will give you generous tips. Male prostitutes can dress the root with their semen."

A MAN-ATTRACTING CANDLE FOR A GOLD DIGGER

Miss Cat of LuckyMojo.com tells us, "To help attract a particular man to you whose name you know, soak Catnip in whiskey or Kananga Water and then sprinkle the liquid on your doorstep every day for 21 days. During the same time light a total of three red 7-knob candles, burning one knob per night, with the name of the man carved onto each knob."

DEACON MILLETT'S SEDUCTION SUGAR BATH

Deacon Millett of FourAltars.org shares an excellent bath to aid in seduction: "Crush a handful of dried Juniper berries with sugar and add a small amount of chopped fresh Ginger root. Gay men add a half-handful of Safflower petals to the mix; women add Roses. Boil a few minutes in water and strain for use in your bath to help heat up your evening."

A HOOKER'S PURSE CHARM TO DRAW TRADE

To draw in tricks, take four pins and pin them through a Five of Clubs so that the head of each pin is toward one of the corner Clubs with its tip pointing toward the center Club, making a large X on the card. Dress the card on all five Clubs with Cleo May Oil and your own sexual fluids. Next, dress a Jezebel Root with Follow Me Boy or Follow Me Girl Oil and your own sexual fluids each day for five days. Then bind or sew the card to the root with red thread and keep this on your person or in your purse to bring in good, calm, kind clients who are generous tippers. This charm can be used by both female and male prostitutes, dressing the root with either vaginal fluid or semen, whichever is applicable.

SWEET AND HOT HERBS TO HELP HEAT UP LOVE PRODUCTS

Add sweet and hot herbs like Ginger, Juniper berries, Cinnamon chips or Cinnamon powder to love-drawing oils, powders, or incenses.

HOYT'S GERMAN COLOGNE FOR SPORTING WOMEN

In 1939, Rev. Harry Hyatt spoke with Madam Wiley, a professional rootworker in Memphis, Tennessee. She had been a reader since she was a child, she said, and most of her clients were White women with love troubles. She said of Hoyt's German Cologne that, "You hear mostly of these sporting women — they've got a bottle of that. They scrub with it for trade. Some of them wash their body with it and then scrub with it."

DRAWING A CLIENT'S MONEY BACK TO YOU

To bring back a regular client's money to you or to turn a first time client into a regular one, take the smallest bill from the cash you received as payment from the client and wrap it up in red paper that you then wet with your sexual fluids. Next wrap all this in green paper and dress it with a money drawing oil, a money drawing sachet powder, and Come To Me Oil. Place a small green candle on top of this packet and light it for 30 minutes each day or once a month during the Full Moon, saying, *"[Name]'s money, come to me,"* repeatedly while the candle burns.

A CHARM TO KEEP A CLIENT COMING BACK

Butch Comer of ConjureButch.blogspot.com tells how to turn a client of a prostitute or a stripper into a regular customer that returns with a compulsion. For this you will need the client's semen, easily obtained by prostitutes, and since men often ejaculate during a lap dance, accessible to strippers, too. Get the semen on a bandana, stocking, or sock. Mix equal parts Cinnamon Oil and Olive Oil together and place a few drops on the soiled item. Wear the dressed item on your right leg with a garter belt for three days to make the client return and spoil you with large tips.

CONTROLLING A MAN WITH HIS UNDERWEAR

A madam from Memphis, Tennessee, told how a woman can make a man desire to always be around her and be generous to her with his money. Get a hold of his used underwear and take the seat out of it. Dress this with Jockey Club Perfume and make a small bag out of it. Put your money in the bag and wear it around your waist and beneath your clothes tied with a cord so it sits close to your vagina. As long as you wear this you will be able to take advantage of him, and he will think more of you.

RAHAB'S BATH TO CLEANSE AWAY SIN

For a prostitute, or one doing dominating lust work, to be purified of sin, add a handful of Hyssop and three tablespoons of Olive Oil to your bath. While standing between two white candles wash downward as you recite Psalms 51, adding, *"Lord, as Rahab was proved a woman of trust and accepted among your people, let me be made clean and accepted, though I sin."* Carry the used water to a crossroads and throw it toward the sunrise, saying, *"In the name of the Father, Son, and Holy Ghost."*

HOLY WATER STOPS THEM FROM CALLING THE LAW
In 1938, Rev. Harry Hyatt interviewed "The Boy-Girl" — a person of ambiguous gender, possibly a genetic intersexual — in New Orleans. The Boy-Girl worked in the hustling life, and explained that if you and your partner are "throwing down White men" — that is, if one of you is jazzing the trick, while the other robs his pockets, then you can ensure a magically safe getaway by throwing Holy Water stolen from a Catholic church on the victim so that he will not be able to report you to the police. Said the Boy-Girl, "Holy Water keeps the law away. No man in high positions today can come where Holy Water is and do evil."

IF YOU GET BUSTED
Miss Cat says, "If you are picked up for soliciting and have to go to court, write the names of all Twelve Apostles on a Sage, Bay, or Plantain leaf, and put this in your right shoe. Write the name of the judge on paper, and put this in your left shoe. Wear these when you go to court. Your date will be delayed, and the third time you go the case will be dismissed."

FIXING THE JURY WITH THE TWELVE DISCIPLES
If you cannot get the charges against you dropped, try this trick, as told to Rev. Harry Hyatt by a worker in Mobile, Alabama, in 1938: The twelve jury members are like the Twelve Disciples, so write the names of six Disciples on one piece of paper and six on another, and put one paper in each of your shoes. This will cause the members of the jury to favour you, as the Disciples favoured Jesus.

TUMBLING THE HOUSE BEFORE GOING TO COURT
The same worker from Mobile who told Rev. Hyatt about the Twelve Disciples in the shoes gave a further spell to use if your brothel has been raided. Just before you leave home to go to court, turn everything in the house over, from your cups and chairs to your mattresses and cushions. You may also turn the mirrors and pictures to the wall. Work of this type is generally called "tumbling the house." Like other inside-out and back-to-front spells, it breaks a jinx and it destroys any link that your enemies may have made to you. Tumbling a house is only carried out on a temporary basis, usually when going to court. It is not a stand-alone spell, but is done in conjunction with other work, as described above.

A HUSTLING WOMAN FROM A PROFESSIONAL HOUSE
In 1938 Rev. Hyatt was in Memphis, Tennessee, when he met "a Hustling Woman from a Professional House." An intelligent, attractive high school graduate driven into prostitution by poverty during the Great Depression, she had been a streetwalker, but now had a secure position in a brothel. She told him many spells of the sporting life. Here are three of them:

A RED LIGHT TO CHANGE A STREETWALKER'S LUCK
"You take the average woman of the streets, her luck gets bad and she wants to bring in more customers," said the Hustling Woman. This is her method: The night before, when you go to bed, about twelve o'clock, burn incense in the four corners of your room. Save the ashes. Get up early in the morning, before any neighbours get up. Put your clothes on — and every piece you put on, put it on the wrong side out. Before you say good morning to anybody, make a fresh floor wash. Start with "good, strong lye-water and the stuff out of your night jar" [your urine]. Add a few drops each of oil of Bergamot, oil of Cedar, and oil of Wintergreen. Put the incense ashes and a pinch of sugar into your scrub water, and scrub your floor, outside your doors, your porch, your steps, and across the sidewalk. Go back into the house and get a red candle and put it behind your door and burn that candle at nine o'clock. Get down on your knees and say your prayers and get up. Keep your clothes on the wrong way till noon. When twelve o'clock comes, turn your clothes the right way, burn some more incense, and "your luck will now be fine — just flourishing."

A PRAYER IS LUCKY WHEN YOU CATCH A TRICK
Wear a Catholic medal or crucifix as a necklace, under your clothes, where it cannot be seen. When you are out on the street, every time you catch a trick, before you go with him, take it out, hold it in your hand, pray, *"Lord, have mercy on me in what I'm about to do,"* and put it back inside your dress. That's lucky and it also brings in more tricks.

THE HUSTLING WOMAN'S FOUR DIAMONDS FOR SAFETY
If you are troubled by the prospect of entertaining violent clients in your room, make a fan of the Nine of Diamonds, Ten of Diamonds, Ace of Diamonds, and Jack of Diamonds, in that order. Tack them up with the faces out above the door to your room to protect yourself.

THE ALLURE OF CLEO MAY

Used by prostitutes and women to attract quick love, both Cleopatra and Cleo May Oil have had an enduring history in hoodoo. The pseudonymous Lewis de Claremont's 1936 book *Legends of Incense, Herb, and Oil Magic* states that, "Today many sporting women (and men) love to use Cleopatra or Cleo May Oil for its alluring scent and subtle entrancing power. They use this wonderful oil as a perfume, rubbing it upon the spot behind the ears, between the fingers, and underneath the arms. It is also said to be very valuable when five drops of this oil are placed upon each corner of the bed that one sleeps on."

FOUR AND JACK OF DIAMONDS FOR WORKING GIRLS

If you are a working girl, hustler, or gigolo and wish to increase your prospects and attract generous clients, dress a Four of Diamonds and Jack of Diamonds with Cleo May Oil. If you work a harder line, dress the cards with Jezebel Oil. Use Q Oil to attract gay customers. A man who works for women can use Mandrake Oil. Tie the fixed cards around a red glass-encased vigil candle that has been dressed with Attraction Oil, light the candle, and pray Psalms 18:19 over it aloud as you do so. Place the candle in a window or near the door of where you work.

MISS CAT'S WORKING GIRLS' LAUNDRY TRICK

"To increase your sexual stamina, encourage reciprocal energy from your clients, and to receive good tips, tie a Dixie John root in a muslin bag and place it in the washing machine with the bedding and underwear that you will use with a client. Once the bedding and underwear are washed and dried, sprinkle a little Cleo May Sachet Powder on them. Use these fixed fabrics to make up your bed and dress in when with clients."

A CAM GIRL'S $2.00 DRAWING BILL

While you are working as a webcam model or cam girl you can help draw viewers to you who will pick you out of a video line-up and give you generous tips by mixing together equal parts of Cleo May Oil, Look Me Over Oil, and Money Drawing Oil. Dress the back of a $2.00 bill that shows the gathered Founding Fathers presenting their draft of the Declaration with a five-spot pattern. Place this dressed bill by or under your camera or in the background where your viewers can barely see it.

FLESH PEDDLERS AND GENTLEMEN OF LEISURE

"Everyone has favourite criminals. Mine are pimps. We can all rob a bank; we can all sell drugs. Being a pimp is a whole other thing."

— Chris Rock

When we discuss matters that do not seem to relate to people's ideas of what hoodoo is about we are often asked, *"What does it have to do with hoodoo?"* How the pimp and hoodoo intersect is an interesting matter. The pimp, like the rootworker, not only has had to skirt the edges of the dominant culture and law, but also seeks to create an environment of independent means. Both flaunt the expected status quo and take authority and power onto themselves without apology. Hoodoo has work to grant mastery, control a lover, increase prosperity and wealth, guard against the police, and empower, all matters that intersect with the aims and means of the pimp. As with all of the sporting life, the difference in experiences between White and Black exists with the pimp, too, and his name has gone from being a slur to a word for wealth, elegance, and style.

PIMPS, LOVERBOYS, AND SUGAR DADDIES

There is perhaps no more controversial figure in the sporting life than the pimp. Admired and reviled, the pimp is a figure who stands out starkly even in a world of glamour, prestige, and power. Although much of what was the sporting life is now legal and even accepted, the pimp remains on the loose periphery, for some an outright criminal and for others a hero worthy of emulation. He has been a figure of deviltry and warning in ways that few madams have, but his influence, image, and boldness makes a stark line in the sporting life and hoodoo for all to see.

The word pimp first appears in English in 1607. It is believed to stem from the French "pimper," meaning to dress up elegantly and from "pimpant," meaning alluring in seductive dress. Pimp used as a verb first appeared in 1636. Pimping is the act of providing a prostitute for sex with a john. The pimp is an agent for prostitutes who collects part, or all, of their earnings. A pimp may receive money for procuring customers, physical protection, or providing a location where his prostitutes engage clients. Like prostitution, the legality of pimping varies by region.

PIMPING AS A CAREER

Pimping is not a "nice" job, and relations between pimps and prostitutes can be abusive. Some pimps employ threats, violence, beating, rape, confinement, psychological intimidation, manipulation, and forced drug use to control women. However, research from the 2010s indicates that the assumption that abusive interactions are the norm is a stereotyped oppression narrative that only represents a small fraction of pimp-prostitute relationships. In fact, it has been argued that the image of the callously violent pimp does not derive from an honest examination of people involved in the life, but is primarily supported by Hollywood screenwriters, contextually questionable trial transcripts, and studies that only interviewed sex workers in situations of prosecution, punishment, or rescue.

Another stereotype holds that mobsters begin their careers as pimps, and indeed, gangland figures such as Lucky Luciano and Al Capone, were pimps when young. However, far more mobsters have started as numbers runners.

It is not uncommon for pimps to leave the life behind and to move into careers as musicians, writers, and entertainers. Pimping requires both charisma and intelligence, and former pimps like Robert "Iceberg Slim" Beck, Clarence "Fillmore Slim" Sims, and Bishop Don "Magic" Juan have shown the world that their talents were not limited to the sex trade.

THE LANGUAGE OF THE PIMP

Established or successful pimps are known as "players." Less respected or newer pimps are "popcorn pimps." Those who use violence to control their girls are "Jonas pimps," while those who use psychology to draw in or keep their girls are "finesse pimps." "Choosing up," is when a pimp takes control of a girl from another pimp, while the loss of a girl to a rival pimp is known as being "peeled." A girl who moves between pimps often is called a "choosey Susie." Informing a pimp that one of his girls has switched pimps is seen as a professional courtesy, and a pimp who responds to this courtesy with aggression is labelled a "gorilla."

Since the 1970s the stereotype of the inner-city pimp has become widespread and given birth to terms such as "pimp walk" and "pimpmobile." The pimp walk is a controlled, affected swagger on one leg that makes one stagger or slightly limp to draw attention. The pimpmobile is a highly decorated, customized, much sought after or admired model of vehicle exhibiting a high status.

THE OPERATION OF THE PIMP

The pimp's main purpose is to maintain a current stable of prostitutes and obtain new prostitutes for his stable. Prostitutes can, and do, move from one pimp to another, but there is a protocol that must be followed. In order to leave one pimp and move to a new one, a working girl must let the new pimp know that she intends to do so. What follows is known as an "intentions period," and during this time the new pimp can reject her. If he agrees to take her in, then he will accept money from her. This cements their business relationship, and he formally becomes her pimp.

Though prostitutes and pimps exist in the United States, this does not mean that prostitution is uniformly legal. Instead, prostitutes work an established part of town, continually vigilant for the police. The pimp often serves as a lookout. If he sees police nearby, he will alert his girls so that they do not get caught. One form of pimping that is legal is the running of licensed brothels in the state of Nevada. Here a brothel owner will employ prostitutes, and men and women can go to the brothel to engage a prostitute's services without fear of legal repercussions. However, Nevada is the only U.S. jurisdiction to allow legal prostitution.

THE PIMP AND HOODOO

The pimp has become a larger than life, almost mythical character, but the pimp lives in a dangerous world surrounded by enemies, rivals, competitors, and police. In such a world any edge helps, and pimps have used personality, intelligence, street smarts, ruthlessness, and hoodoo to gain that edge. The pimp's power to influence others through finesse, style, and sexual potency is legendary, and the use of roots and spiritual work has helped add to and increase those talents. We have police statements from the 1920s and '30s reporting vagrants, panderers, and persons with "no known legitimate business" — all terms for pimps — being arrested while carrying small bags, tins, or containers holding hair, plants, roots, herbs, and oily cloths in them. Though these curios may have confused the White police at the time, it is clear from court records that the items found on these individuals were mojo hands, conjure bags, tobies, and other articles of conjure. Just as a pimp will use hoodoo, so too is he always on the lookout to make sure his rivals, and particularly the girls in his stable, are not using it on him. A pimp catching one of his girls burning a candle on him to control his mind, nature, or generosity will put an end to it immediately.

THE SUGAR DADDY AND THE SUGAR MOMMA

A sugar daddy is a man, a sugar momma being a woman, who offers support, both financial and material, to a sugar baby, an almost always younger romantic or sexual companion. Like a pimp, a sugar daddy must keep a level of control and emotional detachment from his or her companion. Should the sugar baby gain control, she then becomes a gold digger, and the man a chump, a helpless thrall under her Jezebel-like control, making him little more to her than a cash cow. Unlike pimps, sugar daddies operate from a position of economic power. It is they who possess the means by which the sugar baby, gold digger, escort, or gigolo is held.

Relationships between men and women of disparate ages or economic backgrounds are often stereotyped as being sugar parent relationships. These assumptions are rarely correct and often represent jealousy or a lack of tolerance on the part of society to accept relationships containing such differences. Not all sugar baby relationships are solely mercantile; some sugar daddies and their long time companions have developed lasting, mutually emotionally connected, and romantic relationships, with a few even ending in genuine loved-based marriages.

THE LOVERBOY, THE CHICKEN HAWK, AND THE LOTHARIO

Although madams, pimps, and sugar daddies may at times be benign or even philanthropic, a darker element also exists in their world: individuals who viciously exploit children, young people, and the elderly. These are sociopaths and predators, whose behaviour has no excuse.

The loverboy is neither a boy nor a lover. He is a criminal who lures underage girls into prostitution. The loverboy may kidnap, rape, drug, or beat his victims to control them. He may use social media or direct contact to seduce girls to engage in sexual intercourse while being photographed and later threaten them with exposure of the photos. Unless his victims have adequate legal advocacy, the loverboy may get away with charges of having sex with a minor, receive a short sentence, and go on to strike again.

The chicken hawk is a pædophile who preys on young people of either gender. He differs from the loverboy in that his primary motivation is sexual predation, although he may also exploit his victims financially.

The lothario is a seducer of older women, more akin to a grifter than a gigolo. He lures lonely, wealthy women with promises of love or marriage, only to leave his victims heart-broken and financially ruined.

BRINGING THEM IN AND TURNING THEM OUT

A professional prostitute, whether streetwalker, house prostitute, or call girl, can typically pick out one person in her past who "turned her out," that is, who taught her the basic techniques and rules of being a prostitute. How one is "turned out" varies; some enter prostitution on their own without provocation or information from another, some are brought into the life by a prostitute, and some are directly introduced via a madam or a pimp.

Historically, young women were sometimes "turned out" by their own family, either as a sequel to sexual abuse or due to economic hardship. A popular fictional account of this type is found in the 1969 Bobbie Gentry song "Fancy." The song tells the story of a mother turning her 18 year old daughter out so that she can survive the situation described by her mother as *"Pa's runned off and I'm real sick and the baby's gonna starve to death,"* advising her daughter, *"To thine own self be true"* as she goes.

Madams and brothel owners generally prefer not to take on novice prostitutes, some having specific policies against hiring turn-outs. The turn-out's lack of experience can cost the madam or brothel money and clients, and since the training of the novice also requires time and energy, most madams and managers simply chose not to deal with the additional burden.

Pimps, on the other hand, actively engage in turning out girls in order to keep a steady supply for their stables. A pimp or his "bottom girl," his most trusted prostitute, will sometimes operate a "turn-out joint," where novices are taught about "dating johns," collecting money, and making payments to their pimps. Turn-out joints are often organized under the cover of a legitimate business, particularly one that draws in young, attractive women. Former Peoria, Illinois, madam Alyce Broshe, known as Karen Connally, described the operation of her turn-out joint, *"It was a training school. I took in girls, taught them how to dress, wear make-up, how to talk to people."* Once turned out by a pimp, the novice is introduced to his "family," the stable of prostitutes who work for him. Here she may form friendships and engage in rivalries with other working girls as she seeks to rise in position and power.

Hoodoo comes into play not only to help attract girls to a turn-out joint, but also to help keep the law away from it; to help increase the novice's confidence, allure, and draw; and to maintain the girls in the stable as friends or enemies, as might best further the pimp's aims.

HOODOO PRODUCTS FOR PIMPS

The pimp has need of hoodoo in many facets of his day to day life. He may require assistance to help thwart his rivals, quell his enemies, keep the law away, preserve peace among his girls, or simply to give himself a bit of extra spark and luck. All of this is necessary for the dynamic pimp lifestyle, and we list here but a few of the items used to aid in this.

- **Buckeye Nut:** A useful pocket piece to maintain sexual prowess and physical health, as well as to increase one's supply of pocket money.
- **Come To Me:** Designed to attract a new lover of the opposite sex, this formula is used by both pimps and pick-up artists to draw in women.
- **Commanding:** Aids in bringing a girl under the pimp's command, useful in the early stages of the relationship as his control is growing.
- **Controlling:** For control over the actions and thoughts of a pimp's girl, better in the later stages of the relationship once he has command.
- **Do As I Say:** Because the pimp's word is the final say for his stable, this helps increase his influence over his girls to obey his commands.
- **Domination:** Useful to help quell resistance and assert his dominance over one of a pimp's girls, especially when first turning a new girl out.
- **Essence of Bend-Over:** To help the pimp rule over and have his way with his stable, this formula aids him in imposing his will upon them.
- **Follow Me Girl:** Alleged to "make a woman follow you like a Dog," this formula helps pick up artists and pimps to control new women.
- **I Dominate My Woman:** Extremely beneficial in situations where a pimp must gain absolute mental authority over one of his prostitutes.
- **Influence Oil:** Worn by a pimp to help him to influence the thoughts and actions of his girls as well as those he intends to add to his stable.
- **High John the Conqueror:** A powerful pocket piece employed by pimps to draw luck, help gain mastery, and strengthen their nature.
- **Master:** Said to powerfully aid one's ability to control situations and people, this is a good all-around formula for the pimp in command.
- **Pay Me:** Especially helpful when burned on candles to aid in getting back money that is owed to him by one of his prostitutes or associates.
- **Return To Me:** When one of his girls leaves his stable for another or even tries to leave the life, this is useful to help draw her back to him.
- **Rue:** To help combat the glances of his many envious onlookers, the pimp uses this very powerful protective herb to stave off the evil eye.

SPELLS FOR PROCURERS AND PANDERERS

TO CAPTURE A GIRL AND KEEP HER.
To help capture and keep a girl with whom you are already having sex, take your unwashed underwear or one of your unwashed socks and strain some good quality whiskey through it. Give it to the girl to keep for you.

A DOLL-BABY HAND TO CONTROL SOMEONE
Miss Cat tells us to "Cut a piece of root from the sunrise side of a Willow tree just before dawn, name it for the person you wish to control, wrap it in red flannel with Salt, Sulphur, Black Pepper, and a needle. Sew this up, dress it with Hoyt's Cologne, and carry it with you to help control that person."

A PIMP'S MOJO FOR RESPECT, SUCCESS, AND PROTECTION
A gentleman of leisure who wants to have the respect of others, draw success, and protect his back can carry a mojo made of Dragon's Blood, High John the Conqueror, Solomon's Seal root, Five-Finger Grass, and Devil's Shoe Strings in a red flannel bag dressed with Jockey Club Perfume.

FOR MALE VIGOUR AND SEXUAL POTENCY
On a Sunday pour Olive Oil into a bowl and add a pinch of Salt to it. Place a white cloth over it and your head so that it covers you both. While covered, bring the bowl near your lips and pray Psalms 23 over the oil so that your breath falls across it. When finished, remove the cloth, cover the bowl with it, and put the bowl away. Repeat for seven days. After the seventh day bottle the Olive Oil with a whole Ginseng root and let it sit for seven days. Dress your penis with this oil or have a woman do it for you.

HOLD HER TIGHT WITH FINGERNAIL WINE
Back in the 1920s, Daniel Bottler of Atlanta, Georgia, told the folklorist Newbell Niles Puckett that in order to keep a woman with you and under your control, you can trim your ten fingernails and place them to soak in wine, then serve the strained-off wine to her to drink.

FOR RESPECT AND RECOGNITION
To draw respect and recognition, sprinkle powdered up Sampson Snake Root in your shoes; this will assist you in gaining worldly success.

MISS CAT'S CONTROLLING SPRINKLE, MOJO, AND CHEW

"Mix Calamus and Licorice with Commanding Sachet Powder and sprinkle it in the room where you plan to meet someone you wish to control. To dominate in a love affair, add Calamus to any conjure bag filled with love herbs. A man can control a woman if he chews Calamus and spits it on her menstrual blood, either fresh or on her soiled clothing."

A MOJO FOR SUCCESS AND PERSONAL POWER

To make a potent mojo bag to conquer all obstacles, dress a whole High John the Conqueror Root, Master Root, and Sampson Snake Root with Crown of Success and Master Oil. Carry these in a red flannel bag and feed it with Jockey Club or Hoyt's Cologne during the Full Moon.

TO KEEP PEACE AND QUIET AMONG A STABLE OF GIRLS

To help keep a stable of working girls from fussing and fighting among themselves mix Southernwood with Peaceful Home Incense or Peaceful Home Herb Mix and Blessing Incense. Burn it daily on live charcoal where the girls gather; this brings tranquillity and peaceful relationships.

A PIMP'S MOJO FOR SEX AND MONEY

A mojo to aid a pimp in the two most important parts of his business, sex and money, can be made thusly. Take a small red flannel bag and add to it a whole Buckeye Nut, a pinch of Sassafras, an Alligator paw, a teaspoon of Juniper berries, a small piece of Ginseng root, Five-Finger Grass, and a teaspoon of Cinnamon chips. Breathe into the bag before tying it off with nine knots. Dress the bag with a Five Way Aftershave for the Sporting Life (see page 37) or with Hoyt's Cologne, and wear it on you at all times.

A BLACK CAT BONE TO KEEP CONTROL

In "Jim Tampa Blues" Lucille Bogan sings about her pimp, Jim Long, known as "Jim Tampa" and "Mister Tampa Long." He has a stable of tommies, but no matter how bad he treats her, she cannot leave him due to the hold he has on her with a Black Cat bone: *It must be a black cat bone, jomo can't work that hard.* To keep control over a woman so she cannot leave you or get out from under you, dress a Black Cat bone with a controlling oil such as Commanding, Do as I Say, Domination, or I Dominate My Woman. Keep this in a mojo bag anointed with Van Van Oil.

A MAN'S JACK BALL TO ATTRACT AND PICK UP WOMEN

Miss Cat tells us to "Get two small Lodestone chips that "draw" to each other, cover them with Magnetic Sand, and then mould them into a little ball with beeswax. Warm the wax and embed into it a mixture of small High John the Conqueror Root chips, Gentian root chips, and Bo' Hog Root chips. Press these into the sphere and add more warmed wax as you go, until you make a ball about the size of a Walnut. Wrap the finished ball with red sewing thread, making sure to cover every part of it until no wax can be seen. Tie off the thread with nine knots. Place the finished Jack in a red flannel bag and dress it with High John the Conqueror Oil and Nature Oil when you go out to party and pick up women."

MISS CAT'S MALE MOJO FOR MORE SEX

"Men who want to always be ready to please a woman, as well as men who want more sexual activity from their partners or lovers, can mix Johnny Jump-Up leaves together with High John the Conqueror Root chips and Sampson Snake Root chips, and then add three Tonka Beans dressed with their own semen. Carry all this on you in a red flannel bag dressed with a mixture of High John the Conqueror Oil and Nature Oil."

TO CLEAR UP TROUBLE

If there have been fights, fussing, and negative competition among a group of working girls, their pimp or madam can burn dried Pennyroyal leaves on live charcoal as a clearing incense in the home or where they gather. Also, a bowl of Pennyroyal on a home altar next to a bottle of Florida Water helps to keep down squabbling and fighting.

A SEVEN-WAY ROOT BAG FOR MALE LUCK

A very strong mojo for male luck and power is made only with roots and no green herbs. Acquire one small piece each of Peony root, High John the Conqueror Root, Lucky Hand Root, Bo' Hog Root, Sampson Snake Root, Master Root, and Black Snake Root. These seven roots are sewn together into a brown leather bag which is carried on one's person or kept hidden in the home or place of business. To make a similar mojo root bag for female luck and power, use instead one small piece each of Peony root, Queen Elizabeth Root, Lucky Hand Root, Angelica root, Gentian root, Calamus root, and Blood Root in brown leather.

TO KEEP A WOMAN UNDER YOUR FEET

In 1940, a Catholic Spiritualist in Algiers, Louisiana, told Rev. Hyatt how a man can keep his woman under his feet. She said that the man should buy a brand new pair of shoes for himself, carefully pull up the insoles, and write the woman's name on the underside of each insole nine times. He should then lay some Sugar, powdered Cinnamon, and Magnetic Sand in the shoes and neatly replace both of the insoles, using glue to secure them. The woman will be drawn to follow after him, will be very sweet to him, and will bring him her money for as long as he wears those shoes.

TO RULE AND CONTROL A WOMAN WITH THREE HAIRS

In 1939, a man in Waycross, Georgia, told Rev. Hyatt that if you get three hairs of a woman and three Camel cigarettes, thread each hair into one of the cigarettes, and smoke them on three successive days, the woman will be "took in" — that is, seduced or tricked to follow you.

TO RULE AND CONTROL A WOMAN WITH SIX HAIRS

In 1940, a professional rootworker in Louisiana, known as "Nahnee, the Boss of Algiers," gave Rev. Hyatt a way to rule a woman with six hairs. All you have to do, she said, is to write the woman's name six times on a piece of paper, one under the other, from top to bottom. Place three strands of hair from the woman's head and three strands from "the other place" on the paper, and add a pinch of Cinnamon and Sugar — white Sugar for a fair-skinned woman or brown Sugar for a woman of colour. Fold the paper around these items and place it in your wallet. As long as you carry this packet on your person, the woman will have to do what you say, or, as Nahnee put it, when you make the music, she will have to dance.

PROTECT YOUR WOMEN FROM AN UNWANTED VISITOR

Often sex workers at escort agencies, massage parlours, houses of prostitution, or hustling on the street will find that they have attracted the unwanted attention of an unsavoury return customer, a local cop, a nosey neighbour, or some other person whom they wish to keep away from their place of business. To bar such a person from returning, a protective pimp may sprinkle Vandal Root, Black Pepper, and Salt across the front steps of the place and call out the unwanted person's name while commanding that he be unable to cross over it.

TO RULE A WOMAN WITH A WASHCLOTH OR TOWEL

This is one of the simplest, most economical, and easiest tricks to prepare. All it requires is that you and your woman (or women) use the same bathroom, and that you use regular terry-cloth washcloths and towels rather than disposable paper ones. Take a towel or washcloth and wet it slightly. Wash or rub yourself with it, speaking your command, but use no soap at all. Hang it up to dry, and the next person who uses it will get "you" on "her." Depending on what you require of her, you may rub or wash your entire self from head to feet, your face, your hands, or any other body part to which you want the woman to be spiritually connected.

TO RULE A WOMAN'S MIND AND HER SEX

In 1939, the Sumter, South Carolina, root doctor whom Rev. Hyatt called the "Courtroom Specialist" related two ways to rule a woman. The first way controls her mind; the second way controls her sexuality. First, for the mind, you will need a few hairs from her head. These you must burn to ash. Add a pinch of Sugar to this to sweeten her mind. Fold a fresh stick of chewing gum around the Sugar and head-hair ash and chew it. Talk to her and attract her attention while you chew that fixed gum, and she will follow you. Next, to rule her sexuality, get some of her pubic hairs. If you can pull them downward off her body, so much the better, but found ones will do. Burn the pubic hairs to ash, then, using thread or string, tie together four nicely matched pieces of Devil's Shoe String root, no more than four inches long. Rub the ashes into and around the roots. If you carry this charm in your pocket, you will have her nature tied and you can control her.

HOW TO CUT OFF A RIVAL AND DRIVE HIM AWAY

If someone is trying to move into your territory or steal your women, the first thing to do is to try to cut him off. Get an odd number of splinters from a tree that has been struck by lightning. Take them to a fork in the road in his part of town, preferably on a road that leads out of town. A place where the road crosses a railroad line or a bridge is equally good. Stick the splinters there, upright, and call aloud your command for his luck and success to be cut off until he gets out of town. This "quick cut-off" will generally work against a new rival who is spiritually unprepared. If he resists it, you know that he is shielded, protected, or has a worker in his corner, and stronger measures will be needed.

AFTERSHAVES – SHAKE WELL AND DON'T TELL

The image a gentleman of leisure projects is not just about being dominant, sexually potent, and in charge; it is also about looking and smelling sharp and stylish. There are various alcohol-based colognes, perfumes, and aftershaves that have earned a place in spiritual practices and spell-craft which are used in the sporting life, including Hoyt's Cologne and Jockey Club Perfume. These aftershaves and perfumes are fragrances that help give the wearer a needed edge when out and about.

A FIVE WAY AFTERSHAVE FOR THE SPORTING LIFE

This is a good aftershave or cologne to aid one in the sporting life, for luck in gambling, success in money matters, respect from others, making successful pick-ups, or holding sway over the ladies. Soak three pieces of Frankincense, a few High John the Conqueror Root chips, a small bit of Nutmeg, Sampson Snake Root, and a pinch of Five-Finger Grass in a bottle of Jockey Club Perfume. Wear this when going out for business or pleasure.

MISS CAT'S GOOD FORTUNE PROTECTION AFTERSHAVE

"To draw good fortune while preventing anyone from harming you, keep Rattlesnake Master (a.k.a. Corn Snake Root, Sea Holly, or Eryngo) soaking in a bottle of Hoyt's Cologne, and wear this as an aftershave or perfume."

PROF. PORTERFIELD'S POTENT POWER PERFUME

For a perfume or aftershave to help draw women to you like moths to a flame, steep one small piece of Calamus root, Licorice root, High John the Conqueror Root, one whole Vanilla bean, one Cinnamon stick, a pair of Adam and Eve Roots, a small bit of Patchouli, and a few drops each of Crown of Success Oil and Nature Oil in Hoyt's Cologne for one month. Then add nine drops of your urine or semen to fix it to yourself.

MISS CAT'S PROTECTIVE AFTERSHAVE

"Keep a half-handful of Button Snake Root *(Liatris)* soaking in a bottle of Hoyt's Cologne, and wear this as a magically enhanced perfume or aftershave whenever you go out partying, to a casino, or where you might arouse the jealousy of potential rivals or others. On the one hand, it will provide good luck; on the other hand, it will protect you from any 'snakes' who may lurk among your friends, associates, and acquaintances."

SISSY MEN AND BULL DAGGER WOMEN

"Some are young, some are old. My man says sissy's got good jelly roll. My man got a sissy, his name is Miss Kate."

— Gertrude "Ma" Rainey

Those who are lesbian, gay, bisexual, and transgender (LGBT), regardless of race, were a part of the sporting life because of the rejection of them by the mainstream culture. The history of LGBT people in hoodoo is unique because it lays on the dual axis of the gay and Black experience. The expressions and attitudes of being Black and LGBT were, and are, different from the White LGBT experience. Contrary to popular belief, African-American culture has long acknowledged a wide range of gender identities and sexual interests. So widely known was this diversity that mention of it can be found in popular Black music, ranging from Bessie Smith's 1924 "Foolish Man Blues" expressing dislike for *'a skippin' twistin' woman-actin' man'* to Kokomo Arnold's 1934 "Sissy Man Blues," with its happily bisexual affirmation, *"If you can't bring me a woman, bring me a sissy man."*

BOY-GIRLS, QUEERS, AND DRAG QUEENS

Any discussion of same-sex attraction and gender diversity in hoodoo must navigate a doubled history of stereotypes in which evolving social beliefs about gender compete with dominant White stereotypes about Black sexuality. The depiction of people of African descent as beings of unregulated sexuality was bolstered by White slave owners' basely profit-driven obsession with Black fertility, linking supposed Black promiscuity to then-common heteronormative paradigms. Within this framework, Black homosexuality was seen as impossible by Whites because it did not result in procreation. But cross-dressing, same-sex love, and LGBT identities have always been present in Black culture, as shown in old song texts. Waymon "Sloppy" Henry's 1929 "Say I Do It," describes a gay male couple: *"Mose and Pete lived on Greenwillow Street, in northwest Baltimore. Pete run with Mose 'cause he powdered his nose, and even wore ladies' hose."* Lucille Bogan's 1935 "B.D. Woman's Blues" describes bull dagger women who *"can lay their jive, just like a natural man."* These songs and others show a world in which a diverse array of gender identities not only existed, but was commonplace.

BOY-GIRLS

The existence of transgender and intersex people is also found in hoodoo history. Perhaps the most well-known is the "Boy-Girl," who Rev. Hyatt interviewed in 1938 in New Orleans, Louisiana. A person of ambiguous gender, it is not clear whether the Boy-Girl was an effeminate homosexual, transgender, or an anatomical intersexual, but Hyatt believed the latter. The Boy-Girl explained that they were a "freak" because their mother had been hoodooed during pregnancy. They articulated the facts of the hustling life, sexuality, and interracial relations in New Orleans and were a good rootworker as well, having learned from a grandmother. In addition to relating many conjure tricks, the Boy-Girl also spoke about the lives of gay, lesbian, transsexual, and intersex African-Americans.

QUEER THEN AND NOW

Although the word "queer" may make some uneasy, especially those raised in the 1940s, '50s, and '60s, due to its use as a violent term of abuse, "queer" was also used as a playful insider term for those who were "that way." People were "that way" if they crossed the boundaries of what it meant to be male or female, masculine or feminine. "Queerness" had more to do with gender roles than sexual activity. In the '50s "queer" had become an epithet of derision, but by the late '80s many LGBT people began to reclaim the word to describe and talk about themselves in a positive manner. Today the term "queer" is an inclusive term for all types of people and relationships existing outside of heteronormative bounds.

DRAG QUEENS

From the 1920s to the '50s perhaps the most visible queer individual was the female impersonator, or "drag queen." Drag queens had great popularity in gay bars and clubs as well as at "Drag Balls," and during the 1930s many balls were racially integrated under the sponsorship of African-American business owners. Though these events were not specifically gay events, they were attended by Blacks and Whites, homosexuals and heterosexuals, "lesbian girls with their lovers," and female impersonators in great numbers. Drag queens have come to be an integral part of modern gay life for their skewering of traditional gender roles, defying the social norms of male and female appearance and behaviour, and exposing of the artificiality of femininity and masculinity.

ON THE DOWN LOW

Before we begin any discussion about being on the "down low," the first thing we must ask is, "What is the 'down low?'" This is not as easily answered as it may seem, for the down low, or simply the D.L., is a complex and intentionally secretive issue. As the author Keith Boykin explains, *"How do you define someone who doesn't want to be defined? How do you identify someone who doesn't want to be identified?"*

Today saying that a man is on the down low means that he is a man who has sex with other men yet self-identifies as heterosexual. That definition, though, overlooks the history of the term, which has long been used within the African-American community to identify anything secretive or covert, such as a loan, love affair, or illegal business. Only in the past few decades has the term come to be a catch phrase describing African-American men who have wives or girlfriends and also have sex with other men on the side.

This matter gains complexity because many straight-identifying Black men feel comfortable hanging out in Black gay bars, and some homosexual Black men reject the label "gay" as a White homosexual social construct, not because they deny their own homosexual identity, suffer from internalized homophobia, or are on the down low, but instead as a way to create their own identity outside of an often racially insensitive White gay world. Such "out" Black men, while openly admitting that they have sex with other men may describe themselves as "bisexual," or "same-gender-loving." There is yet another twist to the complexity of the down low: the addition of women using the term to describe their own sexual activities with other women.

Some men on the down low are dismissed by openly homosexual men as being "closeted," or as simply "messing around," but closeted gay men are in drag just as much as a female impersonator is on stage, for in their dress, posture, and speech they are impersonating heterosexual men. Gender is performative for everyone, and being on the down low means that one's primary partner, friends, family, and community believe the person, male or female, to be heterosexual. This illusion must be maintained, for once an individual is identified as being on the down low, then that individual is, by definition, no longer on the down low.

So again we are left asking, *"What is the 'down low?'"* The only thing we can clearly say is that the down low is about secrecy in sexual behaviour. You need not be Black, male, or in a relationship to be on the down low. The down low can mean whatever the user wants it to mean.

AS OLD AS TIME

How far back does the down low go? Well, more than three thousand years ago in the first chapter of the Second Book of Samuel, the apparently straight David, the son of Jesse of Bethlehem, says of his friend and rival for the crown of Isræl Jonathan, the son of King Saul, *"Thy love to me was wonderful, passing the love of women."* Earlier, when David was in hiding, Jonathan went to see David, and they *"kissed one another, and wept one with another, until David exceeded."* Saul derides Jonathan for this, *"Thou son of the perverse rebellious woman, do not I know that thou hast chosen the son of Jesse to thine own confusion, and unto the confusion of thy mother's nakedness?"* The choosing spoken of may indicate a permanent choice, and the mention of nakedness suggests a negative sexual suspicion, giving the impression that possibly Saul saw something indecent about his son and David's relationship.

Homosexuality and bisexuality have often been rather difficult for some to understand, but the supposed scandal of a married man sleeping with another man seems tantalizing, and yet inconceivable to many. Nevertheless, the writer Cary Johnson has found clear evidence of homosexuality in pre-colonial Africa, Professor Charles Nero uncovered a centuries-old slave account that reveals the existence of homosexuality among Black slaves, and numerous scholars have documented the impact and influence of Black lesbian, gay, bisexual, and transgendered writers, artists, musicians and entertainers in the Harlem Renaissance of the 1920s and 1930s. It seems, however, that every generation enjoys repeating the drama of this supposed "scandal." Ma Rainey's 1926 song "Sissy Blues" provides one example when Rainey sings, *"I dreamed last night that I was far from harm; woke up and found my man in a sissy's arms."* By 1928 Rainey was no longer on the receiving end, but had moved on to be the operator of the drama in her song "Prove It on Me Blues." Singing of the down low culture of the times, Rainey is the respondent who admits her activity but demands that her accusers *"prove it"* to the world because *"ain't nobody caught me."* It was not only female blues singers who described such matters. In 1930 the openly gay George Hannah's song "Boy in the Boat," told of lesbian women gathering together stealthily on the D.L., *"If you see two women walking hand in hand, just look 'em over and try to understand. They'll go to these parties, have their lights down low, only those parties where women can go."*

YOU SURE GOTTA PROVE IT ON ME

In 1935 when the blues singer Lucille Bogan (a.k.a. Bessie Jackson) recorded "B. D. Woman's Blues," the initials stood for bull dagger. She was telling of masculine or butch women. Other female blues singers, such as "Ma" Rainey, sang of lesbianism and gender roles as well. One of the most famous of her songs is the 1928 "Prove It On Me Blues." In the song Rainey describes how she wore men's clothing, something prohibited at the time by society, and then partied with other women: *"I went out last night with a crowd of my friends; they must've been women 'cause I don't like no men."* In an advertising photo for the record Rainey is pictured enacting the lyrics of the song, standing on a street corner dressed in a jacket, hat, and tie, openly flirting with two women while a police officer watches. The ad clearly shows that Rainey is singing about herself.

One of the most famous lesbians in the blues is not an individual, but a couple: Elvie "Slacks" Thomas (who always dressed in trousers) and her partner Geeshie Wiley. These rural guitarists recorded together and singly, and lived together as lovers for a number of years, surrounded by rumour and mystery, including the possible murder of Wiley's husband.

Lesbian blues songs of the 1920s and '30s describe female and male gender roles and sexuality as being equal or combinable at least 30 years before the modern struggle for lesbian rights. Bisexual and lesbian women, including Bogan, Rainey, Ethel Waters, Alberta Hunter, and Jackie "Moms" Mabley, wrote and sang songs involving same-sex relations, paving the way for later, more "out" performers such as Gladys Bentley, Alberta Hunter, and Big Mama Thornton, who dressed in an openly masculine style. Thornton, who authored the Elvis Presley hit "Hound Dog" is arguably the first blues drag king.

According to the essayist Michele Mitchell, many African-American women in the early 20th century chose to create a "culture of dissemblance." In response to the Jezebel stereotype of African-American women as hyper-sexual, they decided to keep the sexual part of their lives private. Dissemblance went on to become an expected part of proper behaviour by African-American women. Because of this, Bogan, Rainey, Bentley, Thornton, and others' open descriptions of their bisexuality and lesbianism in song was a direct confrontation of the bounds of dissemblance and a refutation of the expectations of White society.

HOODOO PRODUCTS FOR LGBT FOLKS

Most herbs and roots work well for any kind of love, but a few have a special reputation among LGBT workers, and there are hoodoo products, specifically made for LGBT love that have existed for many decades.

- **Banana:** With its phallic shape, it can be used as a proxy and worked on by a gay man to excite great passion and desire in another man.
- **Bo' Hog (Lovage) Root:** This all-purpose love root is especially liked and used by bull daggers who identify as bo' hog or tush-hog women.
- **Catnip:** Traditionally used to draw men to women like a Cat to Catnip, many gay men have also reported great results drawing men to them.
- **Cowrie Shell:** A sacred symbol of the Love Goddesses, its unique vulva-like appearance is dressed and worked to draw a lesbian lover.
- **Cubebs:** Good for drawing a same-sex lover, it is said to make other women receptive to passion and other men both amorous and eager.
- **Follow Me Boy:** Used to aid a gay man in dominating and controlling a male lover, typically used when the lover is someone known to him.
- **Follow Me Girl:** Usually used when the lover is someone known, it assists a lesbian woman in dominating and controlling a female lover.
- **Honey or Sugar Jar:** It is created and worked to sweeten a target to you, whether for love, friendship, or simply to keep the peace in a situation.
- **Hyacinth:** In Greek mythology Hyacinth was the gay lover of Apollo; created when he died, the flower's scent attracts the love of other men.
- **High John the Conqueror:** Useful to enhance the personal sexual power, mastery, luck; commanding, and male nature of a gay man.
- **Lavender:** For good luck in love affairs; purportedly as strong for drawing love from same-sex targets as it is from opposite sex targets.
- **Lavender Love Drops:** Works to draw a lover of the same-sex closer; it can be used both when the target is known or to attract a new lover.
- **'Q' Oil:** The Q stands for Queer; it is widely used by homosexual men to aid in finding passion and drawing love sought from other men.
- **Queen Elizabeth Root:** Good for attracting men for love; numerous homosexual men report success using it to aid in drawing a lover.
- **Sampson Snake Root:** A root of power and strength for straight men, it is similarly used to make Jack-balls and mojos for homosexual men.
- **Safflower:** Called "False Saffron" (Saffron is a love herb), it was used by gay men who tricked as women, but is now a general gay love herb.

SPELLS FOR LGBT PEOPLE

DOMINATION LUBRICATION FOR FIXING A MAN

Rev. Clark shares this lubricating oil to help dominate and rule over your lover. During the Full Moon cycle steep Little John to Chew root, Licorice root, Angelica root, Calamus root, Ginseng root, and an entire bottle of Lucky Swastika Penis Personal Massage Oil all together in a Mason jar. When the Full Moon ends strain the roots from the oil and set them aside. Pour the oil back into its bottle, adding nine drops of your semen. This oil should be used to lubricate your lover's penis. Place the roots you have set aside into a red flannel bag, dress the bag with I Dominate My Man Oil in a five-spot pattern, and keep it hidden on a shelf above head level or behind a picture of your lover. Feed the bag every Full Moon with a mixture of your and your lover's semen.

TO ATTRACT A GAY LOVER

Miss Cat of LuckyMojo.com advises that Safflower petals are "burned on charcoal as an incense by gay men, who smoke themselves with the fumes before going out in search of sexual partners." Additionally, "Dried Safflower flowers and Sampson Snake Root can be steeped in Safflower oil and the oil rubbed on the back of the knees, thighs, and buttocks to attract a male lover."

MISS CAT'S WORK TO KEEP A MALE LOVER FAITHFUL

"Some gay and queer-identifying men will tightly bind together two whole Unicorn Roots with thread and dress this daily with Stay With Me Oil to help keep their male lover sexually faithful and true to them."

ADAM AND STEVE AND ALICE AND EVE LODESTONE WORK

To bring your love to you start this job at the first sliver of the New Moon. Place a pair of either two Male or two Female Lodestones on a mirror, seven inches apart. Dress the Lodestones with Love Me Sachet Powder and High John the Conqueror Oil for two gay men, Queen Elizabeth Oil for two lesbian women, or Lavender Love Drops Oil or Q Oil for those identifying as queer. Each night move the Lodestones closer together. They should be touching on the night of the Full Moon, and your lover will come to you soon after that. Keep the Lodestones touching, and feed them Magnetic Sand and Love Me Oil or Whiskey on every Full Moon.

GAY RECONCILIATION HONEY JAR

When you have done something wrong that caused your lover to leave you, and you wish to bring him back to you, a honey jar can help. On a Friday, fill a lidded jar with honey, to which you add Hyssop, Violet, and Balm of Gilead. Dress a red offertory candle with Reconciliation Oil and place it on top of the jar. Recite Psalms 51, adding, *"David arose out of a place toward the South, and fell on his face to the ground, and bowed himself three times: and they kissed one another, and wept one with another, until David exceeded."* Then make the following vow, *"I will work to bring [Lover's Name] back to me for three months until [date three months from when you begin]. During this time I will attempt to contact him three times, each time with love in my heart and sincere remorse for what I have done. I will accept the results that God gives me."* Then light the candle. Repeat every Friday for three months.

PROTECTION FROM HARM AND GOSSIP

To help protect yourself from the harm and gossip of homophobes, dress a white offertory candle with equal parts Fiery Wall of Protection Oil and Stop Gossip Oil. Roll the dressed candle in a mixture of Kosher Salt, ground Black Pepper, Garlic powder, Alum, and Slippery Elm bark. Pray Psalms 23 over the candle, then light it and let it burn down.

TO KEEP A FEMALE LOVER FAITHFUL

A lesbian or queer woman who wishes to keep her lover faithful will bind together two Queen Elizabeth Roots, one named for herself and one for her lover, with red thread and dress it daily with Stay With Me Oil.

FOR A SAME-SEX PROPOSAL OF MARRIAGE

To help get your partner to propose, first take the Two of Hearts, "the lovebirds," and Four of Hearts, "the marriage bed," from a new deck of cards. On the Two of Hearts write your name over one heart and your partner's name over the other. On the Four, dress each heart and the center of the card in a five-spot pattern with a mixture of Q Oil and Marriage Oil. Dress the Two of Hearts in the same pattern. Place the Four of Hearts face up with the Two of Hearts face down on top of it. Top them with a white 7-knob candle, and burn one knob nightly while burning a mixture of Q and Marriage Incense and praying for a proposal.

A THREE ON THE KINSEY SCALE

For a bisexual woman looking to draw a new partner of either sex, boil some water to which you add a handful of Cubeb berries, Lavender flowers, and Angelica root powder. For a bisexual man, use Cubeb berries, Lavender flowers, and High John the Conqueror Root chips. Steep for seven minutes. Add this to a bath, to which you also add a package of Dixie Love Bath Crystals. Light two red offertory candles dressed with Dixie Love Oil, and place them so that you step between them to enter the bath. Bathe upwards, from toe to head, to draw love to you. Recite aloud Song of Solomon 2:2-3, *"As the lily among thorns, so is my love among the daughters. As the apple tree among the trees of the wood, so is my beloved among the sons. I sat down under his shadow with great delight, and his fruit was sweet to my taste."* Exit the bath between the candles, air dry, and then dress to meet your new lover.

ON THE DOWN LOW AFTERSHAVE

Here is an excellent aftershave for a man who is on the down low and wishes to keep his heterosexual facade intact while seeking sexual interactions with men. Add High John the Conqueror Root chips, a pinch of Violet leaves, a piece of Licorice root, Little John to Chew, Dixie John, Lavender flowers, and Sampson Snake Root chips to a bottle of either Jockey Club Perfume or Hoyt's Cologne and pray Psalms 12 over the bottle. Steep it for at least three to six weeks, shaking the bottle daily.

A DRAG PERFORMER'S POCKET PIECE

Drag queens, drag kings, gender illusionists, and others who engage in gender nonconforming entertainment who wish to help their image and presentation with a little rootwork can carry this lucky pocket piece in their pockets, around their necks on a lead near their bosom, or pinned to their underwear. For a drag queen, tie together a Queen Elizabeth Root, an Angelica root, and a Cowrie Shell with pink sewing thread. For a drag king, tie together a High John the Conquer Root, a Bo' Hog Root, and a Ginseng root with purple thread. Dress the bound-up roots with a half-and-half mixture of Master Oil and Bewitching Oil as the 23rd Psalm is prayed over them. The roots are then placed into a small bag or knotted into a handkerchief; pink for drag queens, white for drag kings, or purple for those who are simply gender nonconforming.

BIRDS OF A FEATHER

Back in the days when being a gay man was an offense punishable by law, a coded term for a male couple was "birds of a feather," which refers to the old English maxim, "Birds of a feather flock together." This phrase can be found, for example, in Waymon "Sloppy" Henry's 1929 blues song "Say I Do It," where *two [men] could be seen, running hand in hand, in all kinds of weather, till the neighbours they began to signify, 'bout the birds that flock together.* What was once a cause of scandal can now be a source of pride: Take two bright and beautiful feathers — those from Parrots or Macaws are excellent — and name one for you and one for your lover or partner. Put a love-drop from each of you on the base of your named feather. Place the feathers in a bottle or bud vase, right out in plain sight. If you are a polyamorous man, you may add a new feather to your "flock" for every man you love, until you have created an entire bouquet of feathers. Be sure to get a drop of the love juice of each man on the base of each feather. The feathers should be individually identifiable, with no two exactly alike, because each represents a specific person. These men will continue to stay in your life as long as their feathers stay in your collection. If someone has to go, remove his feather and cast it to the wind. If there are hard feelings upon parting, burn his feather to ashes and blow the ashes out of your life at a crossroads.

A "DOWN LOW" SPELL TO KEEP SOMEONE COMING BACK

Robert Bryant of New Orleans, Louisiana, shared this simple love-binding spell with Newbell Niles Puckett back in the 1920s: If you take one of your lover's pubic hairs and hide it in a crack in your floor beneath your bed, then as long as it remains there, below you, the person will return to the bed. This type of work can be used to bind a spouse or partner, of course, but due to the placement of the work down on the floor, it seems especially appropriate to bind one who comes to see you on the down low.

TO CONTROL A WOMAN'S SEXUAL NATURE

Cherries and Cherry tree bark are generally associated with women. Miss Cat advises lesbians to "Wrap your lover's picture in a red cloth along with Cherry bark to make her more passionate. If your lover should leave you, then burn the picture, the cloth, and the bark in a hot fire. Your lover's nature will leave her when she is with another."

TO MAKE A MAN FOLLOW YOU

If you are in a house party and see a man whom you would like to hook up with, this sneaky trick may work for you. You will need a bit of absorbent cloth or paper towel, and a glass. Go to the bathroom, wet the cloth or paper and wipe under your arms to get your sweat, then wring the water out into your empty drink glass. Offer to get the person a refill, take your two glasses away, refill the person's glass and drop your sweat-water into it. As the drink is consumed, he will begin to follow you. In 1939 a man in Sumter, South Carolina, told Rev. Hyatt that his mother, a woman of mingled Black and Native American heritage, had taught him this trick 40 years earlier because a bully boy was picking on him. He worked the trick, and it "conquered" the boy, who soon became his best friend and was still following him around to that day. Madame Lindsey, a conjure doctor of Algiers, Louisiana, also told this trick to Rev. Hyatt, the same year.

TWO OLD QUEENS

If the term "two old queens" seems a bit dated, that's because it is. This term for an elderly male couple dates to the era before same-sex marriage was legal. A simple playing card spell helps bring this about. You will need two Queens from a deck of cards. You can pick the favourite suit of each man, choose colour-coded cards (Spades or Clubs for a darker man and Diamonds or Hearts for a paler man), or you may determine the cards by astrological cues (Spades for an air sign, Clubs for a fire sign, Diamonds for an earth sign, and Hearts for a water sign). If the two of you pick the same card (two Queens of Hearts, for example), that is fine; you will just need two decks of cards to get them. Write your names and birthdates on the card backs. Use a bit of honey and your combined sexual fluids to "glue" the two Queens together, face to face. Place the bonded cards in a Bible and consider yourselves wed. May you happily grow old together!

TRANSGENDERED ROOTS

A curio shop keeper who sorts and grades many pounds of roots often finds "transgendered" roots. A naturally formed John the Conqueror Root (a "male" root) that looks like a vulva or a Queen Elizabeth Root (a "female" root) in the shape of a penis are highly valued by intersex or transgendered people. Rare as they are, they are not easy to acquire, but if you befriend a curio shop keeper, and ask nicely, you may be offered one. Use it wisely!

LOVELY LAVENDER LOVE DROPS

Do you know the meaning of Lavender Love Drops? This original formula was first created by Deacon Millett of FourAltars.org and Miss Cat Yronwode of LuckyMojo.com to help engender passion and loving kindness in lesbians and gay men. Not a product for one-night stands, Lavender Love Drops helps bring true, passionate, same-sex love.

A SNEAKY GIFT FOR THE ONE YOU WANT

For a woman who knows the woman she wants, purchase a Cowrie shell and bead necklace or bracelet that you think your intended will like. Dress it with a mix of Lavender Love Drops Oil, Follow Me Girl Oil, and your own vaginal fluid, and state your intent to have this woman be your lover. Give her the necklace or bracelet as a birthday, holiday, or even "friendship day" gift. When she wears it, it will draw her closer.

FOR BRAVERY AND PROTECTION WHEN COMING OUT

To help with worries about coming out to your family or friends, dress a purple or white glass-encased vigil candle with equal parts Lavender Love Drops Oil, Protection Oil, and Crucible of Courage Oil. Light the candle and state your intent to come out, as well as your desire for acceptance and safety. While the candle is burning, wear a mixture of the oils when you go to meet and speak to people to whom you are coming out.

TO IGNITE LOVE BETWEEN GAY MEN

Make a mixture of equal parts Q Oil, Fire of Love Oil, and Lavender Love Drops Oil. Dress a red penis candle with the oil mixture. Take the Jack of Hearts for a younger man, or the King of Hearts for a man your age or older, and write his name across the head of the card and his birth date, if known, across the foot of the card. Lean the card against the candle, then recite Song of Solomon 3:1-4 over the candle and light it.

SEVEN-WAY LOVE HAND

A strong love hand for a gay man is made by adding Catnip, Cubeb berries, Hyacinth, Lavender, Sampson Snake Root, Safflower petals, and a Male Lodestone to a red flannel bag. Breathe into the bag while stating your true intentions, then tie it closed. Smoke it in a mixture of Lavender Love and Attraction Incense, and feed it with Lavender Love Drops Oil.

GAMBLERS, RUNNERS, AND PLAYERS

"The urge to gamble is so universal and its practice so pleasurable, that I assume it must be evil."

— Heywood Broun

Gambling is an ancient pastime enjoyed by most cultures. The act of wagering something of value on an event with hopes of winning thrills something deep within the human psychology. The turn of a card, the toss of a set of dice, the spin of a wheel, the running of Horses and Dogs, and bets placed on every conceivable competition have both made and lost fortunes. Gambling also has within it all the biases and troubles of the larger world. When one goes to find out about famous African-American gamblers there is scant evidence, as if all gamblers were somehow White, until one starts using the word "Mobster" instead. Then suddenly, there is a plethora of figures. The world of the gambler is rife with "lucky practices," hoodoo, conjure, and more, and whether amateur or professional, few take the matter of luck as seriously as the gambler.

POLICY AND THE NUMBERS

One cannot discuss the sporting life without talking about policy, the poor man's racetrack that so many dreams rode on. Policy is an illegal lottery that was first introduced in Chicago in 1885 by the operator "Policy Sam" Young. Policy was run primarily by or for an African-American clientele, and functioned as a de-facto system to redstribute wealth within the community. The game spread rapidly across the country, and by 1901 anti-policy laws started appearing on the books. Despite this, policy flourished everywhere until the 1960s - 1980s, and was only driven out on a state-by-state basis by the new, legal numbers game called "state lotteries."

The name policy may have originated from the street code used by numbers runners or "policy writers" when collecting bets, such as, *"Would you like to take out an insurance policy?"* or *"How much on your funeral policy?"* Policy could also be played at a "policy office" or "policy shop" where bets were taken and the stakes were held.

In New York City, the illegal lottery came to be called "the numbers," and the term used by Caribbean Latin-Americans was "bolita."

SADDLES, GIGS, AND HORSES

Policy bets were placed on groups of numbers from 1 to 78. Popular names for the combinations came from Horse racing. A two-number set was a "saddle," a three-number set a "gig," and a four-number set a "Horse." Gigs were the most popular combinations, but sets of up to 25 numbers could be bet. Popular gig plays had their own pet names. The numbers 3, 6, 9 formed "the dirty gig," the 4, 11, 44 set was "the washerwoman's gig," and so forth. In the 19th century bets as small as one cent a number or three cents a gig were accepted, but by the 1930s the lowest amount one could "invest" was three cents or a nickel. Policy usually paid out at ten-to-one, with larger pay-outs offered for larger groups of numbers.

Winning numbers "fell out" when the operators spun the policy wheel several times a day. Because shady operators could rig their wheels by using magnets, most bettors believed that all of the wheels were "fixed," but despite their distrust, people continued to play. Each wheel had its own individual name, such as "The East & West," "The Interstate," "The Red Devil," "The Dead Row," and "The Streamliner." Some people placed the same bet on several wheels every day; others played only one wheel.

AN HONEST WHEEL

According to Cat Yronwode, "In the 1920s the New York City policy operators tampered with their wheels so often that an 'honest' version of the game was established in which bets were taken on the last three numbers of the daily Federal Reserve Clearing House Report. The company that ran this game, the 'Clearing-House,' was thus immune to charges of fraud and offered the convenience that bettors did not need to contact a runner or return to the policy office to find out if they had won because the numbers were printed in the daily newspapers. In the South another 'on-the-level' game, called 'The Cotton Exchange,' derived its winning numbers from the daily spot prices for cotton on the Chicago Board of Trade. New York's 'Mutuel' got its numbers from the results at Belmont Racetrack.

"At the top levels there were connections between the African-American, Jewish-American, and Italian-American mobsters who controlled these games. They would sometimes team up to open new territories, and other times they killed one another to try and dominate operations in certain cities, neighbourhoods, or among certain ethnic groups. In particular, New York City's Harlem and Chicago's South Side were fought over many times."

CAT YRONWODE ON LUCKY NUMBER DREAM BOOKS

"Dream books, of which *Aunt Sally's Policy Players Dream Book* is the best-known, are part of the African-American hoodoo tradition. They link dream images to divinatory meanings and give numbers for betting. In a typical numbers book, the dream images are listed in alphabetical order with one, two, three, or four numbers beside each item, specifically designed for the convenience of those who bet up to a Horse on policy.

"The authors of these dream books are largely unknown to modern players, but from the 1920s through the 1940s, some of most notable African-American dream book authors included:

- **Professor Uriah Konje (Herbert Gladstone Parris, 1893 - 1972):** A staunch advocate for education and civil rights, he also wrote as Prof. De Herbert Parris. 'The H. P. Dream Book' was his best selling title.
- **Madame Fu Futtam (Dorothy Hamid, 1905 - 1985):** A candle shop owner in New York, she taught spiritual and occult work, as well as giving dream interpretations and lottery luck numbers to her clientele.
- **Black Herman (Benjamin Rucker, 1892 - 1934):** A famous stage magician and a root doctor, his best-known book may have actually been ghost-written by the prolific and mysterious author 'Mr. Young.'
- **Rajah Rabo (Carl Z. Talbot, 1890 - 1974):** Rabo's well-known 'Pick 'Em Dream Book' gives prophetic information in addition to numbers.

"There have been, and still are, many other popular policy and numbers dream books, such as *Billy Bing's Dream Book, Prof. Zonite's Gold Book, Red Star, King Tut's, Three Kings, Kansas City Kitty's, New Gipsy,* and *National Dream Book* — but above them all, *Aunt Sally's Policy Players Dream Book* remains not only the best seller, but also the standard of its class. One now long-lost competitor to *Aunt Sally's* was *The Mystic Oracle, or the Complete Fortune-Teller and Dream Book,* published in 1893 as #21 in *The People's Handbook Series* by F. M. Lupton of New York. In only 32 pages this small pamphlet not only covered Oneirology (divination by dreams) and The French Oraculum or Book of Fate, but it also explained the secrets of such diverse oracular methods as Zodiceology (divination of lucky and unlucky days and hours), Palmistry, Næviology (foretelling by moles, marks, and scars), Cardiology (foretelling by cards, dice, and dominoes), Physiognomy (foretelling from hair and features), Charms, Spells, and Incantations!"

CAT YRONWODE ON HOW TO USE A POLICY DREAM BOOK

"The methods by which numbers were assigned to dream images in the various policy dream books is uncertain. They may have been arrived at arbitrarily, derived from a kabbalistic source such as gematria, or they may have reproduced older European, mostly French, systems of divination.

"How bettors discovered their numbers from their dreams is a question often asked these days. To help readers understand how this was done, and how they can do so, here is an example of dreams and their numbers:

"Suppose you dreamt of a surgeon feeding a Cat and a Dog, and in the dream the surgeon fed the Cat first. When you awoke you would check a policy dream book, in this case *Aunt Sally's* book, and look up the various images: a surgeon, a Cat, and a Dog, and note the given numerical values next to each of them. In this case Surgeon=10, Cat=14, and Dog=4. If you wanted to make a gig wager, you would bet 10-14-4; but if you had dreamt that the surgeon fed the Dog first, then you would bet 10-4-14.

"Some images are given pre-made 2-number saddle combinations and some have 4-number horse combinations, but most dream images are single numbers or 3-number gigs, as these were the most popular types of bets. For example: Butter (some good fortune, but mixed with sadness) 4, 7, 13; Fan (your mistress will be inconstant) 5, 23, 31; Judge (you will overcome an enemy) 28, 50, 70; Ladder (going up, wealth; coming down, poverty) 11, 31, 43; and policy office (foretells riches) 4, 11, 44.

"Not-so-coincidentally, 4, 11, 44, 'the washerwoman's gig,' which signifies both 'lottery' and 'policy office,' is the number-set that Aunt Sally holds on the cover of her *Policy Players Dream Book*. It also appears on the label of a 1930s product called Magic Number Brand Three Number Incense, along with a Black Cat, a four-leaf Clover, a horseshoe, and a pair of dice showing lucky number 7. '4-11-44' was also the name of a musical show by Bert Williams and George Walker, staged in New York in 1899, but despite its auspicious name, the show was a commercial failure. The same gig was later used as the title of the 1926 blues song 'Four-Eleven-Forty-Four' by Charlie Jackson.

"From the 1920s through the 1950s the subject of policy gaming and the number combinations in lucky dream books made their way into blues songs. In the most clever of these songs a series of dream book numbers would be substituted for key words. Jim Jackson and Bumble Bee Slim (Amos Easton) both wrote songs of this type called "Policy Dream Blues."

BEATING THE ODDS

Gamblers, whether they play at cards, bingo, racing, policy, bolita, the lottery, or other numbers games, always want a winning edge to help beat the odds. For this reason they enhance their personal power through the use of amulets, charms, and ritual items to help bring favour and luck.

- **Alligator Foot:** Its "grasping action" makes it a popular key ring charm.
- **Badger Tooth:** An old German-American charm; worn on the left side.
- **Dice Showing Number 7:** A "five-spot" and "Snake-eyes" as a charm.
- **Four-Leaf Clover:** Pressed flat in the wallet to draw money and luck.
- **Horseshoe:** A much loved charm worn by those who play the ponies.
- **Hoyt's Cologne:** Worn as a lucky aftershave while betting or gaming.
- **Money Bag Charm:** A charm shaped like a money bag is good luck.
- **Number 7:** The original lucky number, carried or worn as a charm.
- **Playing Cards Charm:** Worn as a lucky talisman on a charm bracelet.
- **Pyrite:** Iron ore that attracts money and luck; it is carried in a pocket.
- **Rabbit Foot:** Traditional Southern amulet carried as a key ring charm.

UNLUCKY AS LUCKY

Also known as "reversed bad luck," this is the use of unlucky symbols to bring luck and positive results. Unlucky as lucky symbols are used by professional gamblers, gang members, and military personnel. They are frequently found as jewellery and tattoos. Some the most popular are:

- **Ace of Spades:** The notorious "Death Card." Defiant use of this Ace for luck is popular among professional gamblers, soldiers, and bikers.
- **Black Cats:** The supposedly unlucky Black Cat is a popular luck bringer among gamblers, prostitutes, and those seeking social justice.
- **8-balls:** Being "behind the eight ball" means one is in a bad situation, or in a losing position. It is used for good luck, destiny, and respect.
- **Lucky 13:** Thirteen is a lucky number in the sporting life and among Bikers. Those who take risks will wear a charm bracelet of 13 charms.
- **Rattlesnakes:** Favoured by social outcasts, frequently found on Biker and military jewellery such as amulets, belt buckles, or key chains.
- **Skulls:** Used by those who are not averse to calling on the Dead for luck. Gamblers wear skull stick-pins or watch-fobs as lucky charms.

HOODOO PRODUCTS FOR GAMBLERS

From the amateur who spends an occasional day at the races or casino to the serious professional high-stakes poker or pony player, the products in hoodoo for gamblers, luck, and gambling are nearly endless. Whether wearing a lucky scent, dressing or crafting a gambling charm or hand, or dreaming for lucky numbers to wager, there is something for everyone.

- **Algiers:** From the Algiers district of New Orleans, a Fast Luck style formula for bringing general, all-around luck to a gambler with speed.

- **Arrow Root:** An old-time hand-dusting herb powder for gambling luck; combine it with other lucky sachet powders for an extra boost.

- **Aunt Sally's Lucky Dream:** Use these products before bedtime to aid in remembering lucky number dreams to play the numbers or lottery.

- **Black Cat:** A popular dressing oil among gamblers for dressing charms and gambling hands, it is also used for reversing bad luck.

- **Five-Finger Grass:** For success in all the things that five fingers can do, excellent for playing cards, throwing dice, and lottery scratch offs.

- **Huckleberry Leaves:** Traditionally used for dreaming true, they are used by gamblers to aid in inducing lucky number dreams for betting.

- **Lady Luck:** A good luck formula particularly popular among high-stakes card players or those taking serious risks with their wagers.

- **Lucky 13:** Ideal for lottery and bingo players, these products use unlucky conditions to generate good luck and to attract good fortune.

- **Lucky Hand:** Use the root to increase luck in games of chance which call for manual dexterity; use the oil as a hand rub when gambling.

- **Lucky Mojo:** An all-purpose product for gamblers in need of luck; used in many gambling spells or combined with other lucky products.

- **Lucky Number:** An old hoodoo formula, it is helpful for catching lucky numbers to bet as well as to attract good luck and good fortune.

- **Nutmeg:** Used to bring good fortune in games of chance, many gamblers make a powerful lucky charm from it to bring in winnings.

- **Special Dice Oil:** A traditional hand or hair rub oil used by gamblers and crap-shooters; each bottle contains a real pair of miniature dice.

- **Three Jacks and a King:** Frequently worn as a scent or hand rub by gamblers; superb for drawing luck at cards or other games of chance.

- **Van Van:** An old Algiers formula, it changes bad luck to good; worn as a scent or used to feed lucky amulets, charms, and gambling hands.

SPELLS FOR GAMES OF CHANCE AND SKILL

A POCKET PIECE FOR LUCK IN GAMBLING

Wrap a $2.00 bill around a High John the Conqueror Root, a silver dime, and a Lucky Hand Root. Wet the bill bundle with Lucky Hand Oil or with your lover's urine and keep it hidden in your pocket when you go to play cards, shoot dice, go for bingo, or any other kind of gambling.

THE PROFESSOR'S LUCKY 777 GAMBLING HAND

For luck at gambling with cards, dice, or picking numbers, you can make yourself a potent gambling hand using three playing cards. First, take the Seven of Hearts, Seven of Diamonds, and Seven of Clubs from a new deck of cards and dress them with Hoyt's Cologne. Next, get a pair of bone dice, a Rabbit's foot, and a Mercury Dime and dress them all with Van Van Oil. Finally, dress a Lucky Hand Root, a Buckeye Nut, and a bit of Irish Moss with whiskey. Place all of these in a green flannel bag, and breathe into it before tying it shut with seven knots. Dress the bag with Hoyt's Cologne or whiskey and carry it on you when gambling.

CRAP-SHOOTER'S LUCKY HAND RUB

A good hand rub for those who play dice is made by mixing Wintergreen Oil, Rose Oil, and Bergamot Oil in equal parts with Olive Oil. Before you play, rub your hands with this mixture and say the 23rd Psalm.

A CARD-PLAYER'S LUCKY HAND WASH

For a lucky hand wash, boil High John the Conqueror Root chips in water and store. Before you handle cards wash your hands with this liquid.

A GAMBLER'S CHEW FOR DICE PLAYING

Keep a pocket full of Grains of Paradise on you, and chew on them when you go to play, spitting on your hands surreptitiously to dress them.

A LUCKY CLOTH FOR DICE AND MONEY

Butch Comer of ConjureButch.blogspot.com advises that when you gamble with dice, collect your woman's or your own menstrual blood on a piece of cloth and carry it in your right pocket with your dice. Wrap your money in the same cloth, and no one will be able to win it from you.

BATH FOR GAMBLING LUCK

An old-time rootworker from Memphis, Tennessee, told the Rev. Harry Hyatt a quick and simple way to bathe before going out to play cards at night. Dissolve Saltpeter, Sugar, and Blueing in your bath water. Add your own urine, and then bathe downward while saying the Lord's Prayer three times to cleanse yourself. Finally, lightly dress your playing cards with a good luck-drawing oil. The rootworker specified Rose Oil.

MISS CAT'S LUCKY ALL-MINERAL HAND FOR GAMBLING

"A good all-mineral mojo hand for luck with any kind of gambling is made easily by placing a lump of Alum, a piece of Pyrite, and a pinch of Saltpeter in a red flannel bag that is then dressed with Hoyt's Cologne."

A LUCKY GAMBLING MOJO

Miss Cat gives this hand for gambling luck: "Make a mojo of three Crab's Eye Beans fixed with red wax in the hollows of three Alligator teeth, plus three Mojo Beans, and three Black-eyed Peas. Fold these in red flannel and sew it shut. Carry it in a leather bag and feed it with Hoyt's Cologne."

MAMA MICKI'S PRAYER FOR SLOT MACHINE PLAYERS

For those who like to play slots, before playing pray over your money, tokens, or the slot machine Job 20:18: "He hath swallowed down riches, and he shall vomit them up again: God shall cast them out of his belly."

LUCKY LOTTERY MOSS

Keep a pinch of dried Irish Moss in your pocket when you go buy scratch off or lottery tickets or to place a bet at the track or with bookies.

A LUCKY GAMBLING HAND WASH

For a strong hand wash to help bring luck in gambling, first boil a packet of Gambler's Gold Lucky Seven Hand Wash in water and let it steep for seven minutes. Once cooled, strain out the herbs and store the water in a jar. Add a handful of Chamomile to the water and put it away for ten days. At the end of this time mix the water one-to-one with Hoyt's Cologne while reciting the 23rd Psalm aloud. Before you go to gamble wash your hands with the water and cologne mixture while reciting Psalms 119:17-24 aloud seven times, slowly, with absolute confidence and faith.

A DEAD MAN'S BONE FOR GAMBLING LUCK

This gambling spell comes in numerous variations, but as with the many versions of a folk song, although each individual's take on the charm is different, all are in harmony. These were collected by Rev. Harry Hyatt, from rootworkers around the South. They involve going to a graveyard and digging up a finger bone to bring in the winnings:

In 1938, a worker in Memphis, Tennessee, told Hyatt that the lucky gambling finger bone comes from the right middle finger of the dead person and that it is to be carried loose in the pocket.

In 1938 in New Orleans, Louisiana, the bone is a ring finger bone from the left hand, that is, the wedding ring finger. It is ground to dust and combined with a small Lodestone and a whole silver dime. This is sewn (not tied) into a small sack which is set in a saucer of honey and turned over until well soaked. It is then dried and carried as a gambling charm.

That same year, also in New Orleans, another worker said that to make a gambling hand, you take the four tip joints off the four fingers of the right hand of a skeleton, chip them up (do not grind them), and put them into a packet with Lodestone, Magnetic Sand, and six gold-eye needles.

In 1939 in Fayetteville, North Carolina, the bone was the joint of the left middle finger nearest to the hand. Parch it in an oven until dry, grind it to powder, and mix the powder with ashes obtained by burning a Dove's left leg. This mixture is added to a small Lodestone, and the whole is topped off with powder made by grinding silver to dust (probably a silver dime, although that was not stated). Used as a dusting powder or carried as a mojo, this gives dominating power over other gamblers.

In 1939 in Waycross, Georgia, a worker told Hyatt that the finger to use is "the dog finger," by which he meant the index or first finger of either hand. It is to be carried in the pocket.

In 1940 in New Orleans, a worker told Hyatt that it does not matter which bone you get, as long as it comes from the grave of a gambler. Dry the bone and grind it to powder, then blend it with an equal amount of Controlling Sachet Powder, an equal amount of Cinnamon powder, and an equal amount of sugar. (The type of sugar was not stated by this root doctor, but the texture of the mixture is best if you use powdered sugar.) This powder is used to dust your money and tickets when playing bingo or entering raffles in a church. You will control the outcome and the people operating the game will hand you your winnings "with a smile."

MADAME PAMITA'S SPELL FOR THE RACETRACK

Madame Pamita of ParlourOfWonders.com advises this four part working to prepare for a day at the track. First, shower and apply an oil such as Good Luck Oil, Lucky Mojo Oil, Black Cat Oil, or Fast Luck Oil in an upward direction from toes toward head while saying a prayer for luck and prosperity. Second, when you dress for the track dress to create an aura of energy, attraction, wealth, and success. Wearing green or gold can give your money drawing power an extra boost, as well as wearing a lucky talisman such as a small horseshoe or four-leaf Clover. Third, prepare your money by writing "BMW," which stands for "Bring Me Winnings," in the margin of each bill, and then dust the bills with Good Luck Sachet Powder, Lucky Mojo Sachet Powder, Black Cat Sachet Powder, or Fast Luck Sachet Powder. Finally, when at the track visit the Horses in the paddock or the walking ring before each race. Look every Horse in the eye and mentally ask, *"Are you a winner?"* Winning Horses are not skittish or lazy looking and exude an air of royal confidence. Once you have looked at a few Horses, it will be easy to spot the winners, and they will tell you if they are going to go for the win that day. Once you spot the Horse that is ready to win, take a bit of dirt from the walking ring, rub it on your hands with a prayer, and go place your bet.

MISS ROBIN'S LUCKY GAMBLING SPELL

Miss Robin of RobinsMojo.com tells us of a gambling spell she likes to use when going to play bingo. Take a bath the night before you go to play using Pay Me Bath Crystals, and save a small amount of the used bath water. Dispose of it outdoors by throwing it over your left shoulder toward the West, and do not look back. Take all the money that you are going to play with and write, "Money, return to me" or "RTM" on each bill along with your name or initials, and then anoint each bill with Lady Luck Oil, Pay Me Oil, and Money Drawing Oil. Finally, dust the bills with Pay Me Sachet Powder. Get two vigil candles, a Lady Luck vigil candle and a Lucky 13 vigil candle, and dress both candles with a pinch of Pay Me Bath Crystals. Place the prepared bills under both candles, light the candles, and say, *"Let this money bring me more money."* When all of this is done, put some Pay Me Sachet Powder on your chest or bosom and go to sleep that way. Keep the bills under the candles until you go to play, then take them out and use only those bills.

PAYING THE SPIRIT OF A GAMBLER FOR GAMBLING LUCK

During the 1930s, Rev. Harry Hyatt collected quite a number of conjure spells for luck in gambling in which the practitioner pays money to employ the spirit of a dead gambler. To do this sort of work you need first of all to know where a gambler is buried. Second, you must have plenty of cash to spend on this proposition, for you cannot expect the spirit of a gambler to work for you for flowers or kind regards. Here are three regional variations on this spell:

In 1939 Hyatt met a man at the home of H. L. Timmons in Florence South Carolina, who told him that if you are shooting dice, you should get graveyard dirt from the head end of the grave and pay for it, then tote the dirt in the pocket that you carry your dice in. The implication is that the spirit of the gambler will move from his graveyard dirt into the dice and his spirit will direct the dice in their movements.

Also in 1939, in Brunswick, Georgia, Hyatt was told that to win at poker, you can go at midnight to the grave of a woman or a man who was a gambler, open a small hole, take out a pinch of dirt, and pay the spirit in advance by filling the hole with coins, then closing it back up. Wrap the dirt up in a small piece of cloth and place it where you keep your money when you go to play.

A similar spell came from a worker in Waycross, Georgia, that same year. The game was Georgia skin, an old card game, but the style of work was the same. Go to a cemetery at midnight, pay for dirt from the center of the grave, sprinkle it on your pocket change, use the dressed money to stake yourself at the card table, and you will be lucky.

LUCKY LADY GAMBLER'S HAND AND COLOGNE

In 1939 in Fayetteville, North Carolina, Rev. Hyatt learned that to make a gambling hand and a lucky gambling perfume at the same time, you dig from the grave of a woman her two smallest toe bones and her two middle finger bones — all the joints of each — and slip these into a bottle of cologne. (Hoyt's Cologne would be my recommendation for this, due to its reputation for being lucky for gambling.) The bottle with the bones in it may be carried in the purse as a sort of gambling hand, but more importantly, the cologne can also be worn or used to scent a handkerchief while you are gambling, thus bringing the spirit of the lucky lady out of the bottle to lend you a "helping hand."

LUCKY NUMBERS SHOW FOR ME

As the Nicholas Brothers sing in "Lucky Number," "*Oh, give me that lucky number. Hoping that those lucky numbers will show for me.*" Whether it be for lottery, policy, bolita, roulette, the number of the right Horse at the track, or the point spread on a game, lucky numbers and the obtaining of them are an important part of hoodoo in the sporting life.

MISS CAT'S DREAM LUCKY AND DREAM TRUE

"People experienced at games of chance claim that if they dream lucky, then they will have good luck gambling the next day. To dream winning numbers, before going to sleep place a dish of Star Anise seeds on your altar or workspace and burn Star Anise mixed with Psychic Vision Incense."

A LUCKY DREAM PILLOW

Take a Joker from a new deck of cards and write lines of numbers in sequence, "1, 2, 3, 4, 5," across its face until filled. Mix Aunt Sally's Lucky Dream Oil, Lucky Number Oil, and Lucky 13 Oil in equal parts, and pray the 77th Psalm over it. Dress the Joker with the oil mixture and lay it on a piece of green felt. Sprinkle seven crumbled up Bay leaves over this and sew the felt together, making a small packet. Sew this inside a pillow and sleep on it. Each night before going to sleep recite the 77th Psalm and ask the Lord to send you a dream of winning numbers.

PROF. PORTERFIELD'S LUCKY NUMBER FIND SPELL

Write 1 through 9 on a sheet of paper, first in red ink, and then again on the back in green ink, running backwards, 9 through 1. Cut the numbers apart so you have nine small squares, each with the same number on both sides, one green and one red. This is your "Flock" which will bring you lucky numbers. Place your right thumb over each square and pray Psalms 77. Place half a package of Lucky Number Sachet Powder and your "Flock" numbers into a clear, clean jar with a lid. Seal the jar and anoint its lid with Lucky Number Oil. When you want lucky numbers, turn the jar or flask over three times, each time saying, "*Luck is in my favour. Grant me the luck of my desires. My soul is strong in the Lord. Show me the numbers, and I can do no wrong.*" Gently shake the jar. The numbers facing up in green are your lucky numbers. The numbers facing up in red are numbers to avoid. You should not do this more than once a week.

BOOTLEGGERS, TRAFFICKERS, AND PUSHERS

"When I sell liquor, it's called bootlegging; when my patrons serve it on Lake Shore Drive, it's called hospitality."

— Al Capone

How one joins the sporting life is a personal matter. Some are forced in by hard circumstances, others are drawn in by a desire or proclivity they have. There are those who enter for income and livelihood, and a few enter where all of the above meet. They are in the sporting life because they dare to flaunt the law, deliver goods desired by a portion of society, and make their living while doing so. The bootlegger, the trafficker, and to some extent even the fence, hold this corner of the sporting life. Some do this as a way to make an easy living off the dependency of others; however some do it as a form of social protest, seeing the ban on what they provide as being excessive or unjust. As the Mississippi Sheiks sang in 1930 in "Bootlegger's Blues," *"I'd take your worst to go my bail, rather to go to the county jail. You better make it through the world if you can."*

TO LIVE OUTSIDE THE LAW YOU MUST BE HONEST

A classic proverb holds that *"There is honour among thieves."* The implicit concept is one of professional courtesy and adherence to a complete set of in-house rules within a group, band, or guild of criminals working in cooperation. The idea is that even the disreputable and unethical, among themselves, hold to some sort of moral code of conduct.

The converse proverb, *"There is no honour among thieves,"* is used to express dismay that the foregoing system of honour is breaking down or to complain that the greedy nature of criminals interferes in general with their expected code of ethics.

Woody Guthrie said, *"I love a good man outside the law, just as much as I hate a bad man inside the law,"* and Bob Dylan said, *"To live outside the law, you must be honest."* This is the heart of the matter, for if you are going to consider yourself above the rules that society has set, then you had best be very sure you are doing so with the utmost integrity. Those who operate an illegal enterprise must do so honestly, as strange as that might seem. A bad man outside the law stands little chance at all.

WANT SOME WHISKEY IN YOUR WATER

On January 16, 1919, the Eighteenth Amendment of the Constitution was ratified, and a year later, the National Prohibition Act, also known as The Volstead Act, became the law of the land, banning all manufacture, transportation, and sale of alcoholic beverages, except for medicinal and religious use. Almost immediately after the institution of Prohibition in 1920 rum-running and bootlegging began across the United States. Rum-running is smuggling over water; bootlegging is smuggling over land. The term "boot-legging" originated during the American Civil War, when soldiers would sneak pint bottles of liquor into army camps in their boots or beneath their trouser legs. Bootlegging was one of the few professions in the 1920s that was open to all races, and there were notable Black, White, and Asian individuals in the profession. As the well-known California Bay Area newspaper writer Thomas C. Fleming recalls, *"In Oroville, the biggest bootlegger was a Black woman who was in what we called the 'sporting life.' I used visit her son on welcomes, and listen to the console radio she bought him. She always gave him lots of money to spend."*

Under Prohibition the thirst of the nation increased, and in a time when it was scandalous, even teenage girls were openly drinking alcohol. Every city had illegal nightclubs, dance halls, and bars, where patrons could purchase bootleg liquor. Caucasians called them speakeasies or blind pigs, African-Americans termed them juke joints and barrel houses. People took up home-brewing, often according to their cultural backgrounds. Italian-Americans made wine, German-Americans made beer, and, most famously, rural people distilled whiskey from grain. This homemade liquor had many regional names: moonshine, white lightning, block and tackle, mountain dew, homebrew, hooch, white whiskey, bathtub gin, wildcat, or Jake. Unregulated illegal liquor could be dangerously impure, and drinking it might result in blindness, paralysis, or even death. The "Jake Leg" contamination epidemic of 1930, which left 40,000 people paralyzed, is recalled in Ishman Bracey's "Jake Liquor Blues": *"If you don't quit drinkin' that poison Jake you're drinkin', it's gon' leave you with the limber leg."*

When Franklin D. Roosevelt took office in 1933, he kept his campaign promise to bring alcohol back to the public. On December 5, 1933, the Twenty-first Amendment repealed the Eighteenth Amendment, and, in 1936, Bill Cox happily sang, *"Since Roosevelt's been elected, moonshine liquor's been corrected; we've got legal wine, whiskey, beer, and gin."*

GOOD FOR WHAT AILS YOU

During Prohibition, millions of bottles of "medicinal" whiskey were obtained by drinkers through drugstores on real or forged prescriptions. Various industries also were permitted to use alcohol which had been mixed with nauseating chemicals to render it unfit for drinking. This supply was diverted and "washed" of the noxious chemicals. Tap water and flavourings were added, and the result was sold privately, in clubs, or at touring "medicine shows," where unlicensed "Doctors" and "Professors" offered herbal alcoholic tinctures for sale while musicians entertained the crowds.

KICKING THE GONG AROUND

Opium, a resinous extract of the Poppy, entered the demimonde in the 19th century via "opium dens" run by Chinese immigrants, where clients reclined to smoke opium "pills" in pipes held over lamps that reduced the resin to vapour. Some opium dens doubled as brothels. Slumming bohemians could go *"down to Chinatown ... to kick the gong around"* and engage prostitutes in dreamy, languorous sex. For those not near an opium den, laudanum, a medical tincture of opium, could be abused at home. San Francisco banned opium in 1870, and the invention of heroin in 1874 created the first injectable opioid, which in turn was outlawed in 1920. The most famous opium song is "Willie the Weeper," written around 1904 and recorded by many artists, including Frankie "Half-Pint" Jaxon in 1927. By the 1940s, all of the similar songs were about heroin or "junk," not opium. Opium is an almost extinct drug at this time, but modern opioids, such as morphine, codeine, dextromethorphan, oxycontin, hydrocodone, percocet, and vicodin comprise a long list of addictive and potentially fatal cough suppressants and pain relievers still marketed in the underworld.

TAKE A WHIFF ON ME

Cocaine was first extracted from Coca leaves 1859. By the 1880s it was a popular medical drug and an ingredient in Coca Cola. As evidence of its destructive potential mounted, the cocaine was removed from soft drinks in 1903, and in 1922, it was banned. That left a lot of addicts looking for a fix. As Hattie Hart and the Memphis Jug Band sang in 1929's "Cocaine Habit Blues," *"Since cocaine's gone out of style, you can catch 'em shootin' needles all the while."* The 1970s saw a new rise in cocaine use. In both sniffed and smoked forms, it remains a major illegal drug in the 21st century.

SOME SUGAR IN YOUR TEA

In 1910 the nation was gripped by a wave of xenophobia as refugees fleeing the Mexican Revolution entered the country, carrying with them the recreational use of Marijuana. It was at this point that Cannabis began to be referred to as Marijuana, in an attempt to emphasise the drug's "Mexicanness," and raise anti-immigrant ire. At same time, the California State Board of Pharmacy complained that "we in California have been getting a large influx of Hindoos and they have in turn started quite a demand for *Cannabis indica.*" Thus the "Marijuana menace" became an "us" verses "them" matter.

In the 1920s Marijuana found popularity among African-Americans, in part because of Prohibition. Coded "reefer songs" were all the rage, and "vipers" frequented "tea pads" to get high. These establishments were initially tolerated by authorities, but in 1931, the government declared that Marijuana was linked to criminal activity *"primarily committed by 'racially inferior' or underclass communities,"* leading 29 states to outlaw the drug. With liquor again legal after 1933, movie-makers turned to portrayals of the evils of drugs. One such film, the 1936 "Reefer Madness," depicts the "Devil's weed" corrupting a young, susceptible generation. The Marijuana Tax Act of 1937 outlawed Cannabis nationally; it was followed by mandatory sentencing laws like the 1952 Boggs Act and the 1956 Narcotics Control Act. The counter-culture of the 1960s and '70s made Marijuana popular again, but although its rate of use is similar among Blacks and Whites, African-Americans are arrested for Marijuana use at a disproportionately high rate. Currently, the nation is at odds with itself: medical and recreational cannabis is legal in some states, but illegal on the federal level because the 1970 Controlled Substances Act classified it as *"having high potential for abuse, no medical use, and not safe to use without medical supervision."*

WHO PUT THE BENZEDRINE IN MRS. MURPHY'S OVALTINE?

Amphetamine was synthesized in 1887 from the Ephedra plant. Under the name Benzedrine it was first used in asthma inhalers in 1933, and became a drug of abuse by 1939, when people figured out how to dunk the inhaler strips into Ovaltine and drink the liquid. Methamphetamine, known as "speed" or "crystal meth," was synthesized in 1893. During World War Two, soldiers were given Dextroamphetamine to keep them wakeful. Long-haul truckers made "bennies" or "whites" popular in the 1950s and '60s, but when amphetamines are injected, as everyone knows, *"Speed kills."*

KEEPING THE MAN AWAY

In a world where the police can be abusive, dangerous, or even criminal, keeping the law away is not just a concern for those who are actively engaged in illegal activities. People in minority communities, whether racial or economic, must often be wary of legal authorities in their area.

The manufacturers of hoodoo products have had to keep the law off their backs as well. In 1909 the U.S. Post Office began to prosecute mail fraud cases and started strongly targeting merchants of spiritual goods. In response, the makers of conjure supplies had to use disclaimers such as "alleged," "so-called," and "sold as a curio only," writing between the lines about their products in coded language not unlike that used in the demimonde. The need to protect themselves from "the laws" placed spiritual merchants in the sporting life, and in fact, some spiritual workers either were at one time, or still are, drug dealers. Miss Cat Yronwode of LuckyMojo.com, a root doctor who is retired from the Marijuana trade, has supplied us with quite a number of tried and true spells for keeping the law away, or when all else fails, helping to sway a court case in a client's favour.

PEANUTS ON THE FLOOR BRING THE LAW TO YOUR DOOR

Keeping the law away can also be a matter of not drawing the law to you, and when it comes to this, there is an old enemy who brings the law right to your door: the Peanut. The Peanut, also known as the ground nut, is a grain legume, not a nut, and it is a major commercial crop in the United States. Its hulls and skins are said to be very unlucky, and when parched, ground, and powdered are part of traditional War Powder and Drive Away recipes.

The hulls of Peanuts dropped onto the floor of a home are said to cause bad luck and assure that a policeman will come to your house. Peanut hulls thrown on the floor of a gambling house will cause the house to be raided by the police. Older workers will caution one to *"Never throw Peanut hulls around the front door, or you will be arrested before the week is gone,"* and they say that *"Peanut hulls scattered about the door means that you will go to jail."* If the hulls are dropped on the floor of an automobile it will break down, which may explain their sinister reputation in modern NASCAR racing circles. It is also a bad omen for one to come indoors while eating Peanuts. Interestingly, an old term for a workhouse where inmates crack stones is a "Peanut farm."

HOODOO PRODUCTS FOR TRAFFICKERS

Prohibition is long gone, but there are a number of traditional products used in hoodoo for traffickers, smugglers, dealers, runners, or anyone else who finds themselves needing protection while engaging in dangerous work, assistance keeping the law away, or when all else fails, a little extra aid to sway a court case in their favour.

- **Asafoetida (Devil's Dung):** Worn in a bag at the waist to keep police away or burned on charcoal while commanding the law to stay away.
- **Barberry:** Sprinkled in the paths of your enemies to bar their way and stop them following you, it is useful to help get the law off your trail.
- **Black Cat Bone:** The most infamous charm for keeping one unseen or invisible to others, this curio allegedly aids one to travel unobserved.
- **Black Mustard Seed:** To disrupt the activities of unwanted associates or troublesome, meddling people; useful against rivals and the law.
- **Calendula Flowers:** A strong scent, it is used when help is needed to win in court; also powerful to induce prophetic lucky number dreams.
- **Court Case:** It is alleged that these products aid greatly in influencing both judge and jury to decide in your favour when hearing your case.
- **Indian Head Cent:** The Native head depicted on it acts as a "lookout" or "Indian Scout" to help keep Police, DEA, IRS, and other law away.
- **Law Keep Away:** Just as the name explains, this product is used with good results by people who wish to conduct their business in private.
- **Little John to Chew:** A powerful aid to help win in court; a tasty root, it is often prescribed for one to chew it and spit the juice during a trial.
- **Oregano:** A common kitchen herb, it is useful for keeping the law away, protection work, and also a beneficial aid in court case work.
- **Protection Oil:** Said to keep away all harmful influences; a good all-around protection for someone whose line of work is a dangerous one.
- **Road Opener:** For traffickers or smugglers to "clear the path," "open the way," or "remove blockages" when transporting goods or people.
- **Sumac:** If unfortunate enough to have been convicted, this is useful for helping one receive a reduced sentence or fine from the case's judge.
- **Tansy:** A pinch in the shoe or brewed into a tea for a bath guards against the police, DEA, or other inquisitive law enforcement agents.
- **Tobacco:** For success in court cases; mixed with Salt and Deer's Tongue and carried in a pocket to sway a case verdict in one's favour.

SPELLS FOR STAYING SAFE WHILE BREAKING THE RULES

KEEPING A JOINT FROM GETTING ROBBED
To help protect an illegal establishment or a place where illegal goods are stored and keep it from being broken into or robbed, place Solomon's Seal root chips mixed equally with Fern leaves along the window sills.

A RUNNER'S PROTECTIVE MOJO
The worker Shaun Laveau tells of a protective mojo used by those who sell or transport drugs. Place a High John the Conquer Root, a Gator paw, and a Silver Dollar in a red flannel bag and wear the bag over your left breast to keep police officers away from you. If you are making a drug run with a bag, place the three ingredients in the bottom of the bag.

TO KEEP THE LAW AWAY FROM A PLACE OF BUSINESS
Miss cat says, "Determine how many ways there are to enter the place where you conduct your business, and for each way cut an Elder stick five inches long and get a small piece of High John the Conqueror Root. On each Elder stick carve five notches, one-half an inch apart, and then cut a sharpened point on each stick. Drive a hole into the ground about 50 feet down each path leading to the place. Put a piece of High John the Conqueror at the bottom of the hole, and then place the Elder stick with the pointed end down into the hole with the notched side facing North. It is said that no law officer will walk or drive over these Elder pegs."

CHANGE THE BOARDS FOR PROTECTION FROM THE LAW
In 1939, a former bootlegger in Florence, South Carolina, told Rev. Hyatt that to keep the law away, you can go to a cemetery and switch the headboard for the footboard on any grave. (This was in the days when most graves in the South had a tall headboard and a short footboard; you can still find such grave markers in older cemeteries if you look for them.) Call out loud the names of the police or any enemies who might turn you in, and make your wish for protection, *"In the name of the Father, the Son, and the Holy Ghost."* Leave three pennies on the grave and take some of the dirt. Once back home, mix it with Salt and Red Pepper, and sprinkle it around the premises for protection. Like other "tumbled," upside-down, or inside-out spells; this one confuses your opponents and breaks their trail to you.

KEEP THE LAW AWAY WITH THE THREE HIGHEST NAMES

If the police are bothering you, purchase a brand new pack of gold eye needles. Place one needle each outside your house at each corner of the building. Bury them each in a small hole with its head facing up so that the "eye" of the needle can look out for you. As you fill in each hole around the buried needles, say the following prayer: *"In the name of the Father, the Son, and the Holy Ghost, I pray God that the policeman stays away. In the name of the Father, the Son, and the Holy Ghost. Amen."*

INDIAN HEAD CENTS TO KEEP THE LAW OFF

Miss Cat tells a bootlegger's trick: "Nail a row of Indian Head cent 'Scouts' into the threshold or around the door frame of an entrance to keep away the law. You can drill each cent and drive a nail through it or hammer two nails beside each cent and flatten the nails across each other to form an 'X' over the coin, which is said to 'X-out the Laws.' A row of four Scouts is usually sufficient for a home, but nine may be employed where illegal business is conducted, and one old building in the South was found to have 1,500 of them nailed around all the doors and windows! To keep your Scouts watching out for you, dress them once a week with Law Keep Away Oil."

THREE BAGS FOR PROTECTION WHILE CARRYING

For protection from the law while you are transporting illegal goods dress three Indian Head nickels with Law Keep Away Oil. Place one in a small bag with some Black Mustard Seed and wear it in your hat. Place the next in a small bag with some Asafoetida and wear it at your waist. Place the last in a small bag with some Tansy and wear it in your left shoe.

POPPY SEEDS TO DISRUPT POLICE AND COURT ACTIVITIES

Miss Cat says, "Poppy Seeds are a good yard sprinkle to keep away police by confusing them. If you are arrested, carry them in your pocket; confusion will arise in court, and you will go free."

CAT YRONWODE'S LAST-DITCH LAW TRICK WITH SUMAC

"If you have been found guilty in a court case, it is said that you can still help yourself by gathering nine berries from a living Sumac plant. Carry the berries in your pocket when you go before the judge for sentencing, and you will receive a lighter sentence or a smaller fine."

TO KEEP THE LAW AWAY FROM BOOTLEGGERS

A hoodoo woman from New Orleans, Louisiana told the Rev. Hyatt how to make a sweet water to keep the police away. "You use white and brown Sugar because your customers what come around your bootlegging joint — there is some White and some Coloured — and you are doing that to draw your customers. See, you make the water sweet, sweet, sweet and take a glass and put it in. Set it behind your door, and every morning take some of that water in your hand, just a little bit is enough, and sprinkle out your door three times, saying, *'In the name of the Father, Son, and Holy Ghost, let the policeman walk on, keep the policeman walking on, keep him going on,'* and he will not bother you."

FLOOR SCRUB TO DRAW TRADE AND KEEP OFF THE LAW

To keep the law away from a business and stimulate trade in illegal goods in that location, Miss Cat says, "Mix one tablespoonful each of oil of Bergamot, oil of Cloves, and oil of Cedar in a bucket of water and use it to scrub the floors outward toward the front door and onto the sidewalk to drive off intruders. Then make up a wash with one tablespoonful each of oil of Cinnamon, your own urine, and Sugar in a second bucket of water. Use it to scrub from the sidewalk back into the building to draw trade in."

DOCTOR MAGUIN'S FOUR JACKS TO KEEP THE LAW AWAY

Doctor Maguin of Charleston, South Carolina, told Rev. Harry Hyatt that to keep the law away, take the Jacks from a deck of cards and place them at the four corners of the door, then place a penny at the foot of the door, put nine needles across the door, and burn Dragon's Blood Incense.

AGAR-AGAR TO BE UNSEEN OR SEMI-INVISIBLE

When delivering illegal goods, drugs, or stolen merchandise it is helpful to be so inconspicuous that you are virtually unseen by the eyes of those around you. Miss Cat says, "If you hold a bit of Agar-Agar powder in your hand and walk about very quietly, not speaking a word to anyone, then you will go unnoticed even if you are in a crowd."

BLACK CAT'S HAIR TO KEEP AWAY THE POLICE

A worker from Norfolk, Virginia told that to keep the police away you take the hair from a Black Cat's paw and mix it with Back Pepper.

THE "COURTROOM SPECIALIST" TELLS IT LIKE IT IS

In Sumter, South Carolina, in 1939, Rev. Harry Hyatt interviewed a middle-aged male professional root doctor he called the "Courtroom Specialist." Many doctors did work to keep off the law or end court cases, but they did so remotely. This man actually appeared in courtrooms on behalf of clients, and Hyatt said of him, "He is one of the few doctors I met or heard about who actually attended trials." Here are four of his best spells for those who may run afoul of the law.

LAW KEEP AWAY SPRINKLE FOR AN ILLEGAL BUSINESS

Powder together Dragon's Blood resin, Flax seed, Camphor, Salt, manure from a white Horse, and dirt from the foot of a grave; sprinkle this around the building, at the threshold, or in the yard to keep the police away. This sprinkle may also be used on goods that are to be kept hidden at a location away from your home or place of business.

TO GET A CASE DISMISSED OUT OF COURT

Mix Dirt Dauber Wasp nest powder in equal parts with any brand of love powders, Salt, and Pepper. Sprinkle this inside, where the jurors will walk as they enter or exit the courthouse. When the janitors sweep up, they will throw this out and the case will be thrown out because Dirt Daubers, once the young are grown, they leave the nest and never return.

TO GET FAIR TREATMENT IN COURT

When going to court, whether for a hearing, a trial, or sentencing, wear at least one piece of your clothing inside out, carry Salt in at least one of your right pockets, and turn at least one of your other pockets inside out. If you were unfairly accused, this will turn the case around.

TO BE HEARD IN COURT

If you will be called upon to testify during a trial, whether as a plaintiff, witness, or defendant, your voice must be heard and attended to by the judge and jury. Before you leave home, you should pray, saying, *"As Jesus went down to Jordan, so I am going down to court today,"* and ask for God's help. As God said, *"This is my beloved son, I am well pleased; hear ye him,"* so they will listen to you in court. Also carry Devil's Shoe String root on your person and chew it just before you are to speak.

THE "COURTROOM SPECIALIST" VS. THE PROSECUTOR

Due to the nature of his work, the "Courtroom Specialist" of Sumter, South Carolina, had made a study of the ways of county and state prosecutors and district attorneys — and how to foil them. Here are four spells for this sort of work that he gave to Rev. Hyatt in 1939, and they are just as good today as they were then. Remember to put your heart into this work, especially if you are trying to help a client.

TO OVERCOME THE PROSECUTOR OR DISTRICT ATTORNEY

Bind two living Hickory bushes together, call the accuser's name, and stamp down (do not cut down) the bushes, then throw a pinch of Salt on them. On the day of the trial, throw Salt in the direction of the prosecutor's home before leaving your home for court, invoking Lot's wife, who was turned into a pillar of Salt because she looked back.

TO BURY THE PROSECUTOR OR DISTRICT ATTORNEY

Draw a cross in the ground in the middle of a dirt road crossroads, dig a 3" deep trench in the middle, and bury the prosecutor's name in 3" of Salt, stamping on it before you walk away.

TO BREAK THE PROSECUTOR IN THE NAME OF JESUS

On any egg except one from a black Hen, write the prosecutor's name nine times. Cover each name with a large letter "J." Break the egg at a crossroads at 3:00 am. Although the "Courtroom Specialist" did not explain it fully, my friend Miss Cat says that she was taught to "Ask for what you want 'in the name of Jesus' each time you write the letter 'J,' and break the egg 'in Jesus' name, Amen' out loud, stamping your foot as you do so."

TO DOMINATE THE PROSECTOR'S WITNESSES

Cut an upward-pointing stick from near the top of a Willow tree. Go to a cemetery and push the stick into a grave, down to the level of the coffin, three times. Wipe off the dirt with a silk handkerchief. Go to court using the stick as a walking cane and carrying the handkerchief, scented with perfume of any type. When they speak against you or your client, wipe your face with the handkerchief and everyone will become sleepy and unable to listen to opposing arguments; when you are about to speak, take the stick outside the court house and they will wake back up and listen.

THE POWER OF OREGANO

Oregano helps to keep the law away, and in the sporting life it is often used by those involved with Marijuana. Why, you might ask? The answer is simple: Oregano is associated with Marijuana because to the noses of some the two smell alike when smoked, and it has even been used by some dealers as a deceitful substitution. Although Oregano is useful in keeping the law away in general, it is particularly useful for those selling or using Marijuana.

FOR LEGAL AID

If the law does interfere with your work, mix Oregano with Cascara Sagrada bark and Court Case Incense, burn the mixture on charcoal, light brown candles dressed with Court Case Oil, and pray the 35th Psalm for your deliverance every day before your court date so that matters will come out in a way that is most helpful and favourable to your case.

MISS CAT'S MOJO TO KEEP THE LAW AWAY

"Mix Oregano, Fennel seed, and Black Mustard Seed with three chips of Cascara Sagrada bark, and carry them in a blue flannel bag dressed with Law Keep Away Oil when you wish to conduct business in private."

MISS CAT'S SNITCHES-STAY-AWAY YARD SPRINKLE

"Oregano and Fennel are said to keep the law away; Eucalyptus wards off snitches and informers as well. Sprinkle this three-way herb blend once a week in your yard to keep your enemies from telling your business."

KEEP OUT THE COPS

Miss Gat tells us to "Lift a policeman's foot-track and mix it with Oregano, Red Brick Dust, and Black Mustard Seed. Divide this into four parts, and put one part down at each of the four corners of your house. Then, with a Rabbit's foot draw an X-mark at each door, and that will 'X-out the Laws.'"

MISS CAT'S COURT CASE MOJO

"If you oppose others in court, whether as the plaintiff or defendant, write all of your opponents' names on paper, cross them with your name written nine times over theirs, wrap the name-paper around a Little John root, and dress it with Court Case Oil. Place this packet in a bag with Oregano, Calendula, Cascara Sagrada, Dill seed, and Deer's Tongue."

DIVES, HOUSES, AND HOLES

"...I could stay in a cathouse all night. I could eat any place I want...
Get a gallon of whisky, or set in a pool room and play cards or shoot pool."
— John Steinbeck

Whether it was a ritzy club, a hidden-away speakeasy, a luxurious brothel, a warm "crib," a quick hole in the wall, or a down on the luck dive, the sporting life has provided accommodations for rich and poor, for Black and White. Sporting houses have served as the backbone for the hustling life, providing reasonably safe spaces where people could gather for company, entertainment, or to purchase "goods" and "services."

The most public of these establishments amounted to little less than palaces of pleasure, well-known by all. The more private were often hard to find and harder to gain access to without knowing the "right people." For the most part, those who ran these businesses participated in "victimless crimes," supplying prohibited activities and illicit goods to patrons who readily sought them without any need of coercion or trickery.

BROTHELS AND CATHOUSES

Where brothels have existed they have often been a local favourite spot of working men, soldiers, and young men looking for their first sexual experience. They range in price and elegance from the almost unobtainable to the dangerously available. Brothels exist for every taste and proclivity. From the old homosexual brothels, known as "molly houses," to local cathouses, even to the vile "girlery" that specialized in underage prostitutes, there is a bordello to meet the desires of everyone.

The brothel has also been called a "ladies' college," "windowtappery," "hot pillow shop," "heifer den," "school of Venus," and "steer joint." It is not just cat- and whore- that precede the word "house" to denote a brothel, but also: coupling-, fancy-, dress-, grinding-, sporting-, parlour-, hot-, fast-, joy-, and can-. Other prostitution establishments are known as: a chicken-, whore-, or girl-ranch; a house of ill repute; a sporting place or stable; or the more genteel massage or beauty parlour. Whatever they are called, brothels, and the red-light districts that contain them, have earned a prominent place in the world and history of the sporting life.

STORYVILLE

Perhaps the most famous red-light district in the United States was Storyville in New Orleans, Louisiana, which existed from 1897 to 1917. In 1897 the New Orleans City Council passed a municipal ordinance to regulate prostitution and drugs. Alderman Sidney Story wrote the guidelines and legislation to control prostitution within the city, and the ordinance designated a section of the city in which prostitution, although still nominally illegal, was tolerated or regulated. Originally called "The District," its nickname, "Storyville," soon caught on, being an eponym from Councilman Sidney Story. The thirty-eight block area of Storyville was bounded by Iberville, Basin, St. Louis, and North Robertson streets.

Brothels in Storyville ranged from the cheap "cribs," to the more expensive houses, all the way up to a row of elegant mansions along Basin Street for affluent customers. The cribs were 50-cent joints, with the lavish brothels costing up to $10. It was the normal practice of the better Storyville establishments to hire a piano player or a small band, and many famous musicians got their start in Storyville, including Buddy Bolden, Jelly Roll Morton, and Pops Foster. Although Black and White brothels coexisted in Storyville, Black men were prohibited by law from buying the services of prostitutes, either Black or White, from bordellos.

Prostitution was made illegal in New Orleans in 1917, and Storyville slowly changed itself into an entertainment center. The New Orleans city government strongly opposed closing the district; New Orleans Mayor Martin Behrman said, *"You can make it illegal, but you can't make it unpopular."* The District was ordered closed down by midnight on November 14, 1917, after separate Black and White underground houses of prostitution were set up around the city. The district continued as an entertainment center throughout the 1920s, with dance halls, cabarets, bars, and restaurants. Speakeasies, gambling joints, and prostitution were regularly found in the area despite repeated raids by the authorities.

Most of the original buildings in the former Storyville district were demolished in the 1930s during the Great Depression as part of the construction for the Iberville Projects public housing. Today only four remaining buildings from the Storyville period are known to still exist: Lulu White's Saloon, Joe Victor's Saloon, Tark "Terry" Musa's store, formerly known as the Early Saloon, and the Dauphine Orleans Hotel, which was formally the bordello known as May Baily's Place.

THE DAILY GRIND IN A MEMPHIS BROTHEL IN 1938

Rev. Hyatt's interview with "the Hustling Woman" gives us a picture of a Black woman's life in a Memphis brothel. *Warning: graphic language.*

SOME GIRLS

Well, there are some girls won't fool with anything but white trade, and then there're some that use just any of them that come along. Well, naturally, when they catch — when a white man comes in, there's different things that he wants done. Some of 'em like to see French girls.

(They call them French girls. And what do they do?)

They suck the men off.

(I see. What do the others do?)

They want to be whipped.

(What do they want to be whipped for?)

Well, that's their nature.

(Don't they use the girl?)

No.

(I see.)

All you have to do is to remove all your clothes — just pull off all your clothes, you're naked. Take a belt, strap, whip — just anything, and he lays across the bed and you whip him. And some of them you have to talk to like they're little children, and some you have to talk to real rough. And that's their nature. And they'll get through like that and get up and pay you.

(Are there many men here in Memphis that like to be whipped?)

Not very many like that.

(They come in from the country?)

Usually they're traveling men — salesmen from up East — usually like that. But those that's looking for French girls — why the town is run away with them, gang of them.

(What are some of the things the other girls do?)

Well, there's one house around here they call the three-way house. Every girl who lives in that house has to do three things. She has to, you know, just be natural with the men, or she has to be a French girl, or she has to be what they call a corn-hole. A corn-holer — you have to turn yourself up and they use you there behind. Those are about the only three ways.

(You mean all the girls have to do that?)

All of them. In that house, you have to be like that or you don't stay there.

BLUE BOOKS

The "Blue Books," also known as guidebooks, chap books, or sporting guides, were directories of a city's red-light district. The term Blue Book had a shady connotation, and saying that someone was "in the Blue Book" meant that they were a part of the sporting life. From the 19th to early 20th century many cities in the United States had Blue Books, including New York City, Chicago, New Orleans, and San Antonio.

THE SAN ANTONIO BLUE BOOK

The 1911-12 San Antonio, Texas "Blue Book" was a 25¢, 28 page pamphlet with a pale blue cover titled "The Blue Book for Visitors and Tourists and Those Seeking a Good Time While in San Antonio, Texas." The back cover read, *"For Information of the Red Light District Ask Me,"* above a photo of a dapper man, and below it, *"Meet Me At The Beauty Saloon."* The likely publisher, owner of the Beauty Saloon, and irregular police officer was William Keilman. The section "A Straight Steer to the Visitor Within the Gates of the Alamo City, When the Lights are Turned On" dubs the Beauty Saloon a *"safe and sane thirst parlour."*

The Preface reads: *"This directory of the Sporting District is intended as an accurate guide to those who are seeking a good time. To the stranger and visitor while in San Antonio, this book will be welcome, because it puts him on a proper and safe path as to where he may go and feel secure from 'Hold Ups' and any other game usually practiced on the stranger. Anyone perusing this booklet expecting to be regaled with lewd and obscene reading matter will be sadly disappointed, as outside of some harmless wit or toasts it contains only what necessary information is required to make it a directory."* The introduction gives the boundaries of the "reservation," the red-light district of San Antonio. Most of the book's 28 pages are advertisements, including saloons, restaurants, wholesale liquor dealers, a Ballantine's Beer ad, hotels, a drugstore, a bowling alley, a pool hall, livery stables, a taxicab company, cab stands, a bookie joint, and eight ads for "establishments" within the reservation.

The pamphlet also has half a dozen jokes, the "Straight Steer" section which describes saloons, the 1911 San Antonio, Texas League baseball schedule, the addresses of two cockfight pits, a list of Road Houses, and a "Directory Of Houses And Women." In all, over 17 of the booklet's 28 pages are filled with ads connected to the sporting life in various forms.

A, B, AND C LADIES

There are 106 listings in the San Antonio Blue Book, though several give the same address and telephone number. The listings are divided into Class A, B, and C. Class A was $5 and up, Class B $2.50 to $5, depending on the lady in question, and Class C under $2.50 and barter. There are 24 listings for Class A with duplications. 20 listings for Class B, again with some duplication. Every Class A listing had a telephone number. Only four Class B listings are without telephone. Many Class C women shared telephones. This reveals that telephone service was an important part of the prostitution business even as early as 1911. Though 21 entries are followed by telephone numbers, only 9 numbers are listed in the Class C section. Both the Spanish Club at 316 S. Santa Rosa and The Dixie at 209 Matamoras had telephones, but the Spanish Club's was also listed to Adele B. Rice at the same address, while The Dixie's phone was also listed to Belle Wilson, who had the same address as the club. These two women were in all likelihood madams. The remaining 62 listings are Class C. There were a number of one room "cribs" here, but in a number of cases we find women sharing quarters. Anita Dupree and Marian Durant are at 320 S. Concho, Pebble Denman and Ada Davis at 224 S. Concho, May Lomax and "Maxine" at 403 S. Concho, and Sallie Brewer and "Legal Tender" at 216 S. Concho.

Of the 24 Class A listings, 4 are houses or clubs. Of the 20 women, none has a name which reveals ethnicity. Of the 20 Class B listings, there are 4 houses or clubs, and of the 15 women listed by name, only 2 have names that are even vaguely revealing of ethnicity. In Class C only two houses or clubs are listed. Of the remaining 60 listings 12 are definitely Hispanic, while 2, Tama Kato and Sada Yoshima, seem to be Japanese. Around this time there was an influx of ethnic Chinese into San Antonio from the 1910 Mexican Revolution. These two women may have been ethnic Chinese who adopted Japanese sounding names for their work.

Among the ethnically ambiguous names are ones primarily of Anglo origin that may have belonged to White or Black women. The largest portion are of British origin, with French a close second. Many of the French names may be "noms d'amour." The use of these and a faked French accent was popular among prostitutes of the period. Three names, Mary Schwartz, Annie Schneider, and May Burkhart, are possibly German. Two, Vera Meyer and Rosie Friedman, may have been Jewish.

THE JUKE JOINT

A location that stands out strongly in the history of the sporting life in hoodoo is the juke joint, also called a jook joint, barrelhouse, or roadhouse, and, among White people, a honky-tonk. The word "juke" is of uncertain origin but may come from Gullah "joog" or "juk" (rowdy or disorderly), Wolof "jug" (to lead a disorderly life), or Banbara "jugu" (a wicked person). "To juke" is to dance, particularly at a juke joint or to the music of a jukebox, whose name, no longer regional and having lost the connotation of being played in a juke joint, still contains the word.

The juke joint, often found at rural crossroads, catered to the rural work force that began to emerge after the emancipation. Black people were banned from White bars and clubs by Jim Crow laws, and the juke joints represent one of the first "private spaces" for Blacks. Paul Oliver, a writer and historian on the blues called them, *"The last retreat, the final bastion for black people who want to get away from whites, and the pressures of the day."* Juke joints offered drinks, food, gambling, and music for dancing. Some doubled as brothels, a "juke house" being a term once used for a whorehouse. Juke owners also made extra money by selling groceries or moonshine, as well as providing cheap room and board for their patrons. During Prohibition it was common to see juke joints at highway crossings, at railroad stops, and in fields. These were almost never called a juke joint, but rather had such names as the "Black Spot" or "Coloured Café," and often were open only on weekends.

In 1934 the anthropologist Zora Neale Hurston made the first formal attempt to describe the juke joint and its cultural role, writing that *"the Negro jooks…are primitive rural counterparts of resort night clubs, where turpentine workers take their evening relaxation deep in the pine forests."*

Early blues singers like Robert Johnson, Son House, Charley Patton, and many others travelled the juke joint circuit. Here they sang numerous blues songs, including many about hoodoo, such as "The Jinx Blues," "Screamin' and Hollerin' the Blues," and "Hellhound on My Trail."

Rural juke joints gave rise to urban juke joints, often known merely by their addresses, where musicians and singers frequently performed unannounced. Juke joints are still a part of African-American culture, particularly in the Deep South and the Mississippi Delta, although today many feature disc jockeys or jukeboxes rather than live musicians.

HOODOO PRODUCTS FOR ILLEGAL ESTABLISHMENTS

There are a number of traditional products in hoodoo that are useful to aid an illegal establishment. Not only must these businesses overcome the usual rigours of drawing in customers and turning a profit, but they must do so without arousing the watchful eye of the law. They say there's no such thing as bad publicity, but too many raids is bad for business.

- **Allspice Berries:** Commonly used for workings to help bring success, prosperity, luck, and money gained through one's business ventures.
- **Asafoetida (Devil's Dung):** Said to keep off interfering law officers; an ideal ingredient for workings to keep an establishment raid-free.
- **Black Mustard Seed:** Disrupts the activities of unwanted associates or troublesome, meddling people; keep bad customers and the law away.
- **Devil's Shoe Strings:** A strong force to turn back evil, use it to keep unwanted customers as well as the law away from an establishment.
- **Eggshell Powder:** Sprinkle under the front doorstep to keep the police and bill collectors away; particularly potent if from Black Hen's Eggs.
- **Chinese Wash:** Traditional floor wash for attracting customers, particularly to a house of ill repute or private gambling establishment.
- **Elder Flowers:** Most often sprinkled around a property to aid in protection from unwanted criminals, rowdy patrons, and from the law.
- **Fiery Wall of Protection:** Good for general all-around protection of a business from all types of harm, including from rivals and the police.
- **Kosher Salt:** Used for protection and driving away enemies, often mixed with Black Pepper or Sulphur; Salt does what you tell it to do.
- **Law Keep Away:** Commonly used by people who wish to conduct their business in private; ideal for any form of prohibited business.
- **Lodestone:** The bigger, the better; keep it well fed with Magnetic Sand, whiskey, or gold dust to keep the business rolling in dough.
- **Money Drawing:** These products are said to draw money in business; excellent to use in combination with other products for an extra boost.
- **Railroad Spike or Square-Cut Nails:** For nailing down the corner of your property for protection and to keep you from being moved out.
- **Red Brick Dust:** For protection and money drawing, two things every illegal establishment always needs; typically used on the front walk.
- **Wintergreen:** For drawing money and good luck; traditionally used to smoke gambling halls, it is also useful for cathouses and bordellos.

SPELLS FOR DRAWING TRADE TO AN ILLEGAL BUSINESS

TO GET A NEW BROTHEL OR CLUB OFF TO A GOOD START

Miss Cat says, "After cleansing the premises, but before decorating, mix equal parts of Sulphur powder and powdered Ginger and burn them on charcoal in the center of the establishment. Go outdoors while this burns, as it is not safe to breathe Sulphur fumes, and nail a used horseshoe over the front door. The Sulphur will purify the place, and the Ginger will liven it up."

FOUR DIAMONDS TO HELP AN ILLEGAL BUSINESS

In 1938 a practitioner from Memphis, Tennessee, advised the Rev. Harry Hyatt on how to win at illicit gambling and to safely sell illegal whiskey. To do so, tack the King, Queen, Jack, and Ten of Diamonds above your door, fumigate with incense, and clean the place with lye.

BOLDO FOR SAFETY IN PUBLIC HOUSES

Miss Cat says, "Those who operate public places such as bars, restaurants, brothels, and dance halls sprinkle Boldo around the premises once a week to keep away bad customers and those who are intent on doing evil."

IRISH MOSS TO DRAW IN BUSINESS

Mix Irish Moss, Earth Smoke, Wintergreen, and the scrapings from a customer's shoe together and burn it on charcoal to draw customers to your location. Also, Irish Moss may be sprinkled under the door mat or carpets of your place of business to attract generous patrons and clients.

BRING IN CUSTOMERS FOR ILLEGAL GOODS

An old worker from Vicksburg, Mississippi, told the Rev. Harry Hyatt about how one could draw plenty of customers who would keep coming back when selling bootleg whiskey. "Now, you take the High John the Conqueror and a little Lodestone, that is if you kin get hold of a piece, a lady piece, and make you something like a toby — just sew it up in a piece of flannel with silver in it. They say you use a silver dime, and you keep it damp with alcohol. Keep it damp with alcohol all the time, and put it up over your door where your customers come in at. Then that will draw plenty of customers. One will bring the other, and everyone pays his own way, and they will be back again — everyone."

TO DRAW TRADE TO A BROTHEL

To draw in customers to a brothel or cathouse, go to a graveyard, buy a handful of graveyard dirt with a dime, and mix it with equal parts Tobacco snuff and Sugar. Sprinkle this mixture around the front door of the establishment. For an even stronger result, take a bath in water to which you have added a tablespoon of Saltpeter. When you are finished, urinate in the bath, add the Graveyard Dirt, Tobacco snuff, and Sugar. Use this bath water to scrub the sidewalk and steps in front of the house.

MISS CAT'S WASH TO DRAW TRADE TO A WHOREHOUSE

"On a Friday morning build a fire outdoors and burn a man's worn-out left shoe with a pinch of Sugar. Put the shoe ashes, your own urine, and a tablespoon each of Ammonia, Salt, and Sugar into a bucketful of water. Mop with this from the sidewalk inward to attract men to the house."

LUCKY BROTHEL BUSINESS SMOKE

On a Friday night mix together a few scrapings from the left sole of a man's shoe along with Wealthy Way Incense Powder, Cinnamon chips, and Sugar. Burn this on charcoal to attract customers for the weekend.

PROTECTION SCRUB FOR AN ILLEGAL BUSINESS OR HOME

Miss Cat says, "Wash your doorstep with a bucket of water, add your own urine, then sprinkle Red Brick Dust on the doorstep. To make this scrub stronger, write the name of the captain of the police on paper, burn this name-paper to ashes, and add the ashes to the scrub water."

FOR HUSTLING AND BOOTLEGGING

A worker in Memphis, Tennessee, told Rev. Hyatt a way to draw luck for hustling and bootlegging. She said that if you are living a hustling life, get up early in the morning and urinate in a bucket. Do not let anybody else urinate in that bucket. Take it and scrub the porch with it. Then on Fridays, get some oil of Bergamot and put about two or three drops of it in a bucket of hot water. Mop the house on Friday with it, and that draws luck for bootlegging and hustling, too, but you must not speak to anybody until twelve o'clock. Do not have anything to say to anybody when you get up and mop your house. And also on Monday mornings do not let women folk come into your house because it is bad luck to you.

DRAWING CUSTOMERS TO A BOOTLEGGER

A worker from New Orleans, Louisiana, told Rev. Hyatt how to bring a crowd to your house if you are bootlegging. Take nine pods of Red Pepper and three ounces of Sugar, ground-up Nutmeg, and Ammonia, and put that in your water and make a floor scrub. Then you get some Fast Luck Oil and put it in there. Take your broom and sweep all in the corners of the house. Never sweep the dirt out the front; always let everything go to the back. And then, when you use that water you scrub with, you always carry it all to the back. And as soon as you are done, you take the beer or a little wine, and you put some of that in the water and scrub again. But let your scrubbing always go toward the back door.

FOR A SUCCESSFUL BUSINESS

To draw customers to a business, first take a Ten of Clubs and write the success sigil "$$¢¢$$" at the top, middle, and foot of the card. Burn the card to ash, reciting the 114th Psalm as it burns. Collect the ashes from the card and mix them together with a packet of Money Drawing Incense Powder and equal parts powdered Irish Moss and Earth Smoke. Divide the mixture in half, then sprinkle half of the mixture around the front door of the business and outside along the sidewalk in front of the place. Burn the second part of the mixture over live charcoal in the mornings before opening up for the day, reciting the 108th Psalm aloud as you fumigate inside the store with the smoke from the burning mixture.

SIX DECKS OF CARDS TO BRING TRADE TO A BAR OR CLUB

In 1939 a professional root doctor in Sumter, South Carolina, advised Rev. Hyatt on how to draw business to a beer garden, piccolo joint, or juke joint using the ashes of a deck of cards, which he called a "paire."

"If another fellow opens up right next to you to beat you out of business, and you want the trade to come into your business instead and to be successful, just buy yourself six paire of cards, real gambling cards, and burn up three paire of them. Hide the ashes of the three burned-up paires under your counter. Place the three unburned paires on top of the ashes, side by side, and on top of each paire place a silver coin. You need three pieces of silver, even if it is just three dimes. This will help to draw trade to your business. But remember, when you go to sweep out your business, never sweep those ashes or cards out. Just leave them where you hid them."

GUARDING THE CORNERS

When one runs a business involved in the demimonde, whether it be a gambling hall, casino, brothel, bar, or strip joint it is desirable to keep the establishment not only safe and profitable, but also peaceful. An excellent way to accomplish this is to dress the corners and center of the establishment to make sure to bring in all the good things you need.

FOR A PEACEFUL AND LUCKY JOINT

To help keep a place of business you are running that caters to customers who may become rowdy or start fights, and keep luck moving your way, mix three teaspoonfuls of Wintergreen essential bath crystals, one named for "The Father," one for "The Son," and one for "The Holy Ghost" into enough Peace Water to fully dissolve it. Shake this up while reciting Psalms 4 aloud and then dress the four interior corners and center of your establishment with the mixture.

DRESSING A BROTHEL OR STRIP CLUB FOR LUCK

A good way to help a brothel or strip club stay profitable and lucky is to mix together a teaspoonful of Algiers Bath Crystals, a pinch of Tobacco snuff, 9 drops of Attraction Oil, and a small quantity of your morning urine into Rose Water. Shake well and dress the four interior corners and center of the business with the liquid every nine days.

TO KEEP A GAMBLING HALL SAFE

Places where gambling is conducted are vulnerable to raids by the police or robbery by thieves or the clientele. To help protect an establishment or room where gambling is carried out, mix laundry blueing and powdered Solomon's Seal root chips into holy water that has been stolen from a Catholic church. Pray the 91st Psalm over the mixture and then dress the corners and center of the room or establishment with this.

KEEP IT EASY BAR

To help keep a bar or club where illegal activities such as gambling, prostitution, or trafficking are conducted safe from the law, ill fortune, or bad luck involving police informants, mix 3 drops of Lady Luck Oil, 7 drops of Law Keep Away Oil, and 9 drops Rue Oil into Florida Water. Use this mixture to dress the four interior corners and center of the bar.

THE DRAW OF CINNAMON
Cinnamon powder and bark are both used to bring good fortune with money, business, and gambling. They bring good winnings and those looking for high-stakes games, and they draw trade straight in the door. In the sporting life numerous prostitutes have gone by the working name "Cinnamon" to evoke an image of being sweet yet spicy-hot. As an essential oil it is one of the popular scents used to mask the smell of sex when a prostitute must engage one client after another. Its strong and biting smell has been used in an attempt to cover the scent of drugs, such as Marijuana. This, and the fact that its sharp, sweet smell has a reputation as being a "love scent," has also made it a popular incense in the sporting life.

MISS CAT'S INCENSE FOR A GAMBLING HALL OR CASINO
"To smoke a gambling hall or casino to help draw in customers and money, make a mixture of Cinnamon, Cloves, Camphor, Wintergreen, and Money Drawing Incense, then burn the mixture over live charcoal."

MISS CAT'S INCENSE FOR AN ILLEGAL BUSINESS
"To draw in customers to an illegal business and at the same time keep the law away, mix chopped up Devil's Shoe Strings, crushed Dragon's Blood resin, and oil of Cinnamon, and burn it on charcoal. As it burns carry it to each corner of the house and also the windows and doors."

TO DRAW TRADE TO A BROTHEL, BAR, OR DANCE HALL
Miss Cat says, "On Mondays, Wednesdays, and Fridays, get up before dawn without speaking to anyone and mix Red Brick Dust, oil of Cinnamon, Love Me Oil, and Van Van Oil into nine buckets of water and scrub from the sidewalk toward the door."

TO BRING BUSINESS AND KEEP THE LAW AWAY
To keep the law away from, and ensure a steady cash flow into, a business involved in the sporting life, place a mixture of Irish Moss, Cinnamon powder, Sugar, and Law Keep Away Sachet Powder under the entrance mat to the establishment in a five-spot pattern. Each morning burn Money Drawing Incense and Law Keep Away Incense in the building, and once a week dress the doorway of the premises with an equal parts mixture of Money Drawing Oil and Law Keep Away Oil.

DRESSING FOR THE DEMIMONDE

"I wanna go home and I ain't got sufficient clothes, doggone my bad luck soul; wanna go home and I ain't got sufficient clothes;"
— Blind Lemon Jefferson

The sporting life is not just a matter of actions, behaviours, and endeavours, it is also a matter of image, style, and flair. The gambler, pimp, working girl, madam, pickup artist. and those in LGBT communities of colour are all known for their panache, verve, and class, whether it be in speech, movement, or dress. The sporting life has long been a place where those who were not "proper" were thrown, but those in the life did not simply suffer under the rod of "proper people's" judgement. They have claimed and embraced their place and identity vigorously, distinguishing themselves openly in public by their make-up, hair styles, clothing, and ornamentation. From the zoot suits, pompadours, and dangling watch-chains of previous eras to the tattoos, piercings, and body modification so popular nowadays, the style and glamour of the sporting life shines on.

NICE SHOES AND THE WALKING BLUES

Most Americans see their footwear as an extension and expression of themselves, and up until recent years one's shoes were an immediate indicator of one's social and economic standing. Shoes not only affect our perceptions of others and ourselves, but also our ideas of maturity and strength. Not only does footwear act as an extension of self, but also as a storehouse of history, memory, and meaning. It may seem strange to some people these days to place such importance on shoes since "everyone has shoes," but it was not so long ago that many people did not have good shoes, or even shoes at all. Even these days the purchasing of children's shoes can be a major economic burden for many families.

Sharp looking shoes play a significant role in the sporting life, with a cool cat being judged by the quality and upkeep of his shoes. As Harold Koda, curator of the Metropolitan Museum of Art's Costume Institute, says, *The foot is the pimp for the shoe.* Shoes also figure prominently in folk magic and hoodoo, as well as in the Bible. *"How lovely are thy feet with shoes, oh prince's daughter,"* reads the Song of Solomon 7:1.

ALL GOD'S CHILDREN GOT SHOES

Before and during the Civil War era in the United States, White working class people often went barefoot from Spring to Fall. They sometimes had shoes for school and church, but they did not wear those shoes unless necessary. Before commercially made shoes became readily available many people did not have a pair of shoes of their own until their teens. By the mid-1800s the industrialization of shoe making allowed most people the ability to afford shoes of their own, and for the first time different patterns of the right and left shoe were standardized. The situation was very different for African-Americans during the same period, as necessities like shoes were a rarity in the slave quarters.

One of the best examples of this is found in the old protest spiritual commonly known as "I Got Shoes," or "Heav'n, Heav'n." The song is a brave condemnation of slavery, with the singers boldly confident that an ultimate justice exists as they insist that *"all God's children got shoes,"* as well as robes, harps, and crowns! The lyrics go further, calling out that *"everybody talkin' "bout Heav'n ain't goin' there,"* emphasising the hypocrisy of the slave owners who went to church every Sunday, talked about Jesus and Heaven, but then returned to the plantations and farms where they oversaw and profited from a distinctly un-Heavenly lifestyle that ran on the slavery of human beings, enforced through physical, emotional, and sexual abuse.

The unknown author of "I Got Shoes" expressed a sense of outrage, and yet hope, for an entire community. The song reverses the power hierarchy of the time, for God's children will have a place in Heaven, but the others *"ain't goin' there."* Of course Heaven might not only be a new life in the world to come, but it could also be a life away from slavery, slave owners, and the plantation; it could be a life of safety in the Northern states, the West, or even Canada.

Long after the days of slavery and "I Got Shoes" passed, shoes continued to play an important social role. Until the 1960s going around barefoot marked one as being not only poor, but also common. During the '60s many local laws were passed against going barefooted in public in response to the rise of the unshod flower children. Men and women, especially those in the sporting life, were judged by the condition of their shoes. A gambler of any import would not be caught dead at the track in scuffed shoes, and a pimp in worn-out shoes was a worn-out pimp. At the end of the day it is hoped that all God's children do, indeed, have shoes.

PUT ON YOUR MADISON BLUES SHOES

To see the importance of shoes in African-American culture, one need not look further than the blues. Blues lyrics are full of shoe references: their importance, the lack of them, and how their state of upkeep reflects on the singer. Tallahassee Tight (Louis Washington), Joe Evans, and Black Bottom McPhail all caution about the need to hide your money from unscrupulous women in the bottom of your shoe. In Georgia White's "Walking the Street," from 1936, the singer explains that, as a streetwalker, she has *"got to make six dollars to buy my man a pair of shoes."* Lucille Bogan, in1930's "They Ain't Walking No More," laments that *"tricks ain' walkin' no more"* because *"I need shoes on my feet."* Singers bemoan the infidelity of lovers for whom they had bought shoes; for instance, in 1927's "You Gonna Quit Me Blues," Arthur "Blind" Blake protests, *"Give you my money, honey, to buy your shoes and clothes."* Elmore James, in 1960's "Madison Blues," told folks to *"put on your Madison shoes."* And when Carla Thomas called Otis Redding "country" in 1967's "Tramp," it was because of his *"big ol' brogan shoes."* Good shoes have always meant good days and an end to the walking blues.

FEAR NOT TO WALK OVER EVIL

As society shifted from a barefoot one to a shoe clad one, so too did hoodoo shift to include the use of shoes. To understand why shoes are so crucial in hoodoo, it helps to know how important foot-track spells are in African-derived magic. Conjure is rife with spells in which practitioners lay down tricks against others by placing powders, cross-marks, or bottle spells in or under their paths so that they will step on the mess and be "poisoned through the feet." The agent that conveys negative work, such as a jinx, may be a sprinkling of Goofer Dust, Hot Foot Powder, Crossing Powder, Jinx Powder, Rattlesnake skin powder, an "X" made with stones, or buried nails or pins. Negative foot-track magic like this can cause bad luck, unnatural illnesses, and serious medical problems; and the victims of this kind of hoodoo are said to be "hurt" or "poisoned through the feet." People use various protective substances and formulas to guard against being hurt by stepping in such messes, including Salt, Pepper, Fear Not To Walk Over Evil Powder, and Jinx Killer Powder. The latter two can be used preemptively to protect pathways as well as the feet, the stockings, and, of course, the shoes.

HIDE MY EYES

If the eyes are the window to the soul, then sometimes one needs to close the shutters and draw the drapes on those windows. Sunglasses, or sun cheaters, have existed for centuries, and their first use was not to protect the eyes, but to hide them. In the 12th century sunglasses made from panes of flat smoky quartz, which offered no corrective aid but protected from glare, appeared in China. Chinese documents tell of judges using such sunglasses to hide their eyes while questioning witnesses. "Smoked glasses" were also worn for various medical reasons beyond correction of poor vision. During the 19th and early 20th centuries amber, green, and brown-tinted spectacles were often prescribed for those suffering from light sensitivity, such as that brought on as a symptom of syphilis.

In 1929 Sam Foster began mass-production of sunglasses made from celluloid. He sold them under the name Foster Grant out of a Woolworth's store on the Atlantic City Boardwalk, where they caught on quickly among beach goers. In 1936 Polarized sunglasses became available when Edwin H. Land made lenses incorporating his patented Polaroid filter. By 1937, 20 million pairs of sunglasses were sold in the United States, and in 1938 *Life Magazine* proclaimed that sunglasses were a *"new fad for wear on city streets... a favourite affectation of thousands of women all over the U.S."* Aviator sunglasses were all the rage during World War Two. Mirrored sunglasses hit the market in 1948. At that point, sunglasses had become a matter of fashion, with new models introduced yearly.

Sunglasses are worn for many reasons besides fashion. They make eye contact impossible and hide one's emotions. The avoided eye contact can suggest that the wearer is detached or cool. Sunglasses are popular with police and pimps for intimidation, with those in mourning to hide grief, and with gamblers who play card games to hide "tells" that their eyes might give away to other players. Women who are abused wear sunglasses to hide their bruises; drug users wear "teashades" to hide their bloodshot eyes or the dilation that Marijuana or heroin causes to the pupils.

Those in the life of magic and mysticism use sunglasses, too. This is seen in 1940s ads in popular hoodoo curio catalogues, such as King Novelty and DeLaurence, which used to offer sunglass as spiritual protectors. One late ad for the DeLaurence "Wise Boy" Mirror Sun Glasses tells how they offer "double protection" for one's eyes and one's soul.

WITH HIS EYES SHADED

The famous rootworker and hoodoo Doctor Buzzard of Beaufort, South Carolina, was well-known not only for allegedly being the "greatest rootworker of all time," but also for his distinctive purple lensed glasses that he wore constantly. Perhaps because of the fame of Doctor Buzzard's work and his distinctive spectacles, other hoodoo workers began to be reported wearing coloured spectacles, lenses, and later sun cheaters. The wearing of sunglasses can offer a worker some protection when he or she is out in public as well. They help shield and shade one's eyes, offering protection from the evil eye. Blue-tinted sunglasses work well for this, as do mirror shades which reflect back evil or negativity thrown at one just like a mirror. Also a pair of sunglasses can be cleansed, blessed, and then dressed with appropriate protective oils or powders in small amounts to help make sure that those wearing them are safe from harm while on the streets. My good friend the late Dr. E., Eduardo "Eddy" Gutiérrez, may his memory be a blessing, advised that if you wish to have success when doing a piece of work on a picture of someone, make sure that the person in the picture is not wearing sunglasses.

WATCH MY HAT

Stylish hats have been a part of the sporting life for both women and men, and hats, like shoes, say much about their wearers. The economic and social status, the image, and the intentions of men and women can all be read from their hats. A finely made chapeau can be expensive, particularly these days when the milliner and the haberdasher are rare. Those who have a good hat will make sure their hat does not get taken by mistake. My grandfather carried a small business-sized card in the inner brim of his hat that read, *"Like hell it is! This hat belongs to Charles Jones!"*

It is not just a matter of losing one's hat in a case of mistaken hat identity, either, for a hat also is a potent personal concern, and men will jealously guard their hats from falling into the hands of strange women. The hat has a long history in folk magic, and most know to never lay one on a bed, as it brings bad luck. Hats can be fixed or dressed to aid, harm, or control the wearer, and any man who lets a woman walk off to the restroom while in possession of his hat deserves everything coming to him. Finally, the spiritual value of covering one's head is well-known in many cultures, and a hat can protect you from more than just the Sun.

HOODOO PRODUCTS FOR CLOTHES AND PERSONAL CARE

Undoubtedly looking sharp and feeling confident in your appearance is an important part of the sporting life. Those who wish a little aid in gaining that extra edge of confidence or who want to attract attention, love, or luck can find it in the listings here. Careful, though — being on top of your game also means protecting yourself from envious onlookers.

- **Angelica Root:** To provide strength to women and bring them good health and protection; the whole root is popular as a pocket piece.
- **Attraction:** Alleged to attract money, love, luck, success, or whatever you desire; mix it with the drawing condition oil of choice for a boost.
- **Bewitching:** To make an impression or draw friends and attention; oft used as a personal scent of mystery, fascination, and sexual allure.
- **Black and White Skin Soap:** A high-quality, traditional African-American beauty bar, it is also used in works for interracial dating.
- **Crown of Success:** Many people anoint their head with this oil or add it to hair products for special financial, school, or career success.
- **Fast Luck:** Reported to bring rapid luck in matters of money, love, and business; when you need results now and have no time to wait.
- **High John the Conqueror:** To enhance personal sexual power, mastery, and luck for men; the whole root is popular as a pocket piece.
- **Hoyt's Cologne:** A cologne widely reputed to bring great good luck to gamblers; it is also used to dress mojo bags and gambling charms.
- **Look Me Over:** Used in countless glamour spells to attract attention, mainly from men; wear it to get admiring glances and to be noticed.
- **Power Oil:** Believed to increase your personal strength and spiritual power; good to help boost your confidence and control of your life.
- **Prosperity Oil:** To increase your income and lead you to a better life. Use this oil to help you get ahead in money matters and in business.
- **Protection:** To keep away all harmful influences; great for all-around protection from your enemies and jealous rivals who wish ill on you.
- **Reversing:** Used to send jinxes and curses back to the one who sent them; superb to protect against the evil eye or anything thrown at you.
- **Van Van:** Said to change bad luck to good and to open the way to new opportunities; traditionally worn by many as a perfume or cologne.
- **Wealthy Way:** A product for your lifestyle; to keep a continuing, unending, easy stream of spending money. Not for emergency cash.

SPELLS FOR LOOKING GOOD AND STAYING SHARP

MISS CAT'S PROTECTIVE SHOE-POWDER
"Mix dried and powdered Seneca Snake Root with any brand of foot powder. Dust your feet and the inside of your shoes with this, and no tricks laid in the dirt along your way can harm you, for you will walk shielded."

A SHOE PAPER TO FORCE SOMEONE TO DO AS YOU SAY
A worker out of Savannah, Georgia, told that to force someone to do as you say, take a pencil and write your target's name out on a plain piece of brown paper. Fold that paper toward you as you say, *"In the Name of the Lord, Name of the Father, Son, and Holy Ghost."* Place the paper under the insole of your shoe and wear it. Wear the paper every day, and you will just be able to conquer that person any way that you want to.

SHOE TRICK FOR STRENGTH AND ENERGY
To keep up your energy, dust ground-up Master of the Woods and Sampson Snake Root in your shoes and pray the 23rd Psalm over them.

PROTECTIVE POCKET SQUARE
Those who wear a good suit will make sure they have a good pocket square for their suit jacket's front pocket, but nice clothes can bring envy and the evil eye from others. An effective protection against this is to carry a pinch of Anise seed knotted up in your pocket square. This can be made more effective by adding to it Agrimony or Rue and a Cat's Eye shell.

SHOE PROTECTION FROM GOSSIP AND SLANDER
Miss Cat says that you can "Burn Slippery Elm to ashes and use the ashes to draw a cross on the bottoms of your shoes. This will allow you to walk among gossips and slanderers and not become the target of their loose talk."

SILVER DIME TO WARN OF EVIL WORK
It is a very old practice to wear a silver dime in your shoe or at your ankle as a lucky charm and a warning against enemy work. If you step into some mess that an enemy has laid out for you of Goofer Dust, Hot Foot Powder, or Crossing Powder, all of which usually contain Sulphur, the coin will turn black due to a chemical interaction, and you will know.

EXCITE A MAN'S LOVE WITH HIS CLOTHES

Miss Cat says, "Sprinkle Queen Elizabeth Root powder on your clothes and on the clothes worn by a man you love, then you will be able to produce a strong love for you on his part. A little of this powder can also be mixed into his food or drink, along with your menstrual blood, vaginal fluid, or a bit of your urine to help attract the man's sexual interest.

CALMING YOUR ENEMY SHOE SPELL

On a piece of paper write out the names of the 12 Apostles. Below their names write Matthew 5:44: "But I say unto you, Love your enemies, bless them that curse you, do good to them that hate you, and pray for them which despitefully use you, and persecute you." Below that, write name of your enemy. Fold up the paper and place it in your shoe while reciting Psalms 34:14: *"Depart from evil, and do good; seek peace, and pursue it."* Step firmly into your shoe while calling on the Father, Son, and Holy Ghost. That will conquer them under the teachings of Jesus Christ and bring them down easy. As you walk, you are stepping on their heads, but you are bringing them under the control of the Lord.

MISS CAT'S TRIPLE STRENGTH LOVE DRAW

"To help attract new love and romance, place a Violet leaf in your left shoe and wear it that way for seven days. At the end of those seven days place a new, second Violet leaf in your left shoe and wear it again for seven days. Finally, place a new, third Violet leaf in your left shoe and wear it that way for one last seven day period, for a total of twenty-one days in all."

MADAME NADIA'S GOLD DIGGER'S BODY SCRUB

Madame Nadia of MadameNadia.com gives this recipe to attract those who are interested in showering you with gifts and supporting you financially: "Mix together half a cup each of white Cane Sugar and Safflower Oil, one and a half tablespoons Goldschläger, a pinch each of Calendula, Five-Finger Grass, and Catnip if you are a female or Calamus if you are a male. Add to this two drops of Sweet Orange Essential Oil, two drops of Chamomile Essential Oil, and a dropper-full each of Follow Me Boy or Follow Me Girl, Look Me Over, Bewitching, and Cleo May condition oils. Work everything together, and then use it to scrub your body from foot to head to draw in sexual fascination and financial generosity."

PLAYING CARD IN YOUR SHOE FOR STEADY WORK

If you need steady work, first get a white crucifix candle, two blue offertory candles, and the Ace of Clubs. Draw a dollar sign in the two blank corners of the card, sign your name at its top, and write the words "Steady Work" over and over across the card until it is filled. Dress the candles and card with Steady Work Oil. Place a pinch of Gravel Root or Steady Work Sachet Powder on top of the Ace of Clubs, place an overturned white saucer over it, and set the crucifix candle on top of the saucer. Place the three candles in a row, with the blue ones to either side of the crucifix candle. Light all three candles, pick up the blue offertory candles in your hands, pray the 23rd Psalm aloud, and ask for a job. Replace the blue candles to their previous places and let all the candles burn until they go out. When you leave for a job interview, take the Ace of Clubs from beneath the saucer and place it inside your right shoe along with the name of the company or the business card of your interviewer, so that you will "walk on them" during the interview. Keep a Steady Work vigil light candle dressed with Gravel Root and Steady Work Oil burning at home in a safe place while you are at the interview. Carry some Gravel Root and a pinch of Salt in your pocket, and during the interview remember to look the interviewer in the eye as you speak.

PROTECTIVE SHOE SPRINKLE

To shield yourself where you walk, in case someone has thrown for you, sprinkle a mixture of equal parts of any three of the following four ingredients into your shoes: Salt, Saltpeter, Red Pepper, or Black Pepper.

TO ATTRACT A LOVER

To help attract a new lover, pray Psalms 89 three times daily for nine days after 6:30 a.m. As you do so, anoint yourself over your heart with Come To Me Oil. On each of the nine days as you prepare yourself to meet a new special someone burn three teaspoons of Come To Me Incense on charcoal and place some Attraction Oil on your neck or wrists. On the fifth day of the work write out five different letters of the alphabet, representing possible names of new lovers, on five small slips of paper, and dress them with either Follow Me Boy or Follow Me Girl Oil, depending on your desires. Place one slip in each shoe and the others in your clothing. Look your best, and get ready for a new lover.

FROM THE NECK UP

It might seem that you need only mind your shoes, feet, and pockets, but one's head, hair, and eyes can also benefit from a little protection, or be a path toward manipulation by others, depending on the situation. These works are sure to help keep your chin up and your eyes forward.

MISS CAT'S OLD-FASHIONED HAT TRICK

"If a woman loves a man more than he loves her, she can ask to wear his hat, either in playfulness or because of the weather. Once she has his hat, she should pretend that she needs to go to the bathroom. While out of sight, she should pull down her pants and rub the hat between her legs. After that, she should give the hat back, and he will love her more."

MISS CAT'S "HOW TO KEEP A MAN THINKING OF YOU"

"Put one of your pubic hairs into the sweat band of his hat when he is not looking, and as long as he wears that hat, he will always think of you."

MADAME NADIA'S "LASHES TO DIE FOR"

Madame Nadia of MadameNadia.com gives us this recipe for women or transgendered women to help them look good and attract and draw male lovers. "Mix one part Queen Elizabeth Powder with two parts baby powder or loose translucent powder. Coat your lashes with one coat of your preferred mascara. Then press a bit of the powder mixture into your lashes, from below, with a small, flat make-up brush."

PROF. PORTERFIELD'S PROTECTIVE MIRROR SHADES

To help guard you against the evil eye, as well as to reverse and reflect back evil others throw on you while you are out in the world, get a pair of comfortable sunglasses; blue-tinted, mirrored, or polarized lenses are best for this work. Mix Reversing Oil, Protection Oil, and Fiery Wall of Protection Oil together in equal parts and add a pinch of Crab shell powder. Shake the mixture up seven times as you pray the 37th Psalm aloud. Dab a small amount of the oil mixture onto a soft, clean, white cloth and carefully apply the oil to the frame, rims, nose, and ear pieces of the sunglasses, then rub a tiny bit across the lenses and clean them as you pray the 52nd Psalm aloud. Wear your dressed shades whenever you are out and where others may have ill intentions toward you or your luck.

BIBLIOGRAPHY

ALLEN, Irving Lewis. *The City in Slang*. Oxford University Press, 1993.

BOYKIN, Keith. *Beyond the Down Low: Sex, Lies, and Denial in Black America*. Carroll & Graff, 2005.

CAMPBELL, Helen, Thomas Knox, and Thomas Byrnes. *Darkness and Daylight or, Lights and Shadows of New York Life*. A.D. Worthington & Co., 1892.

DEVI, Debra. *The Language of the Blues from Alcorub to Zuzu*. Billboard Books, 2006.

DITMORE, Melissa Hope. *Encyclopedia of Prostitution and Sex Work, Volumes 1 and 2*. Greenwood Press, 2006.

DRAKE, St. Clair and Horace R. Cayton. *Black Metropolis: A Study of Negro Life in a Northern City*. Harcourt, Brace, 1945.

ECKHARDT, C. F. "San Antonio's Blue Book." TexasEscapes.com/CFEckhardt/San-Antonios-Blue-Book.htm. Texas Escapes LLC, 2006.

ELLINGTON, George. *Women of New York the Underworld of the Great City*. Ayer Co. Pub., 1869.

FOSTER, George G. *Celio: or, New York Above Ground and Under-Ground*. Dewitt & Davenport, 1856.

GREEN, Jonathon. *The Cassell Dictionary of Slang*. Cassell, 1999.

HEYL, Barbara Sherman. "The Madam as Teacher: The Training of House Prostitutes." *Social Problems* 24 (5):545-555. May 1977.

HOEKSTRA, Dave. "The Happy Hustler: Bishop Don "Magic" Juan isn't really a pimp anymore — but he still gets to look and act like one." *The Chicago Reader*, 2011.

HURSTON, Zora Neale. *Mules and Men*. J. B. Lipincott, 1935. Reprinted, Harper Collins, 1990.

HYATT, Harry Middleton. *Hoodoo – Conjuration – Witchcraft – Rootwork*. [Five Vols.] Memoirs of the Alma Egan Hyatt Foundation, 1970–78.

LAFOREST, Aura. *Hoodoo Spiritual Baths*. Lucky Mojo Curio Co., 2014.

MARCUS, Anthony, et al. "Conflict and Agency among Sex Workers and Pimps: A Closer Look at Domestic Minor Sex Trafficking." *The Annals of the American Academy of Political and Social Science,* May 2014 vol. 653 no. 1 225-246.

MICHÆLE, Miss and Prof. Charles Porterfield. *Hoodoo Bible Magic: Sacred Secrets of Scriptural Sorcery*. Missionary Independent Spiritual Church, 2014.

MILLETT, Deacon. *Hoodoo Honey and Sugar Spells*. Lucky Mojo Curio Co., 2013.

NEWTON, Esther. *Mother Camp: Female Impersonators in America*. Prentice-Hall, 1972.

OTTLEY, Roi. *Inside Black America*. Eyre and Spottiswoode, 1948

PETRIK, Paula. "Capitalists with Rooms: Prostitution in Helena, Montana, 1865-1900." *Montana: The Magazine of Western History* 31.2 (Spring 1981) 28-41.

PORTERFIELD, Prof. Charles. *A Deck of Spells*. Lucky Mojo Curio Co. 2015.

RUSSELL, Thaddeus. *A Renegade History of the United States*. Free Press, 2010.

SULLIVAN, John Jeremiah. "The Ballad of Geeshie and Elvie." *The New York Times,* 2014.

THOMPSON, Nathan. *Kings: The True Story of Chicago's Policy Kings*. Bronzeville Press, 2003.

WILSON, James F. *Bulldaggers, Pansies, and Chocolate Babies*. University of Michigan, 2010.

YRONWODE, Catherine. *Hoodoo Herb and Root Magic*. Lucky Mojo Curio Co., 2002.

----------. *Paper in My Shoe*. Lucky Mojo Curio Co., 2015.

----------. *Blues Lyrics and Hoodoo*. LuckyMojo.com/blues.html. Lucky Mojo Curio Co., 1994-2016.

----------. *Southern Spirits: Ghostly Voices from Dixie Land*. Southern-Spirits.org, 1994-2016.

----------. *Aunt Sally's Policy Players Dream Book*. LuckyMojo.com/auntsallys.html. Lucky Mojo Curio Co., 1994-2016.